NAVIGATING MOTHERHOOD

Jordan-
May the Lord bless
you at every turn as you
mother. He is for you
and He is with you!

Becky Brooks

NAVIGATING MOTHERHOOD

BECKY BROOKS

bel esprit books
Dallas | Fort Worth

Navigating Motherhood: Finding Your Way By Following Jesus
Becky Brooks

Copyright © 2020 Becky Brooks

Published by Bel Esprit Books, LLC
PO Box 821801
North Richland Hills, TX 76182

Cover and interior design and typesetting: Kent Jensen | knail.com
Author photo: Kelly Warnock | Revelation 4:11 Photography

ISBN: 978-1-7331734-5-2

First Edition: August 2020

To all the women who have come through
the Navigating Motherhood Class.

Your love for the Lord and your children challenged
and blessed me weekly. I will always be thankful
for the time we shared.

---

*"May God give you every desire of your heart and
carry out your every plan* as you go to battle. *When
you succeed, we will celebrate and shout for joy. Flags will fly when
victory is yours! Yes, God will answer your prayers
and we will praise him!"*

Psalm 20:4-5 (TPT)

CONTENTS

INTRODUCTION

One of the things I love about motherhood is the bond it creates. Having children brings you into an instantaneous sisterhood. There have been many times I have only just met someone, and suddenly we are swapping stories of childbirth, potty training, and recommendations for which cream works best on a rash. Then at the end of the conversation, we might actually introduce ourselves. See, our names aren't always shared before the bonding begins. All that matters in that moment is what we have in common: both of us turn our heads when a child calls, "Mom!"

For years, everyone who has benefitted from the Navigating Motherhood class curriculum has had some personal connection to me. They have been in the class I taught or heard me speak at their church. With the birth of this book, *Navigating Motherhood* has the opportunity to travel places I have not. Because of this, I want to share the story of how it all began.

In 2012, the women's minister at our church had a vision for a study that would draw in young moms. Our numbers showed that our semester studies always started off strong, but our attrition rate was substantial. As we asked young mothers about that trend, they mentioned that due to the unpredictability of children and the stage of life they were in, they would often miss a day in their workbook … and that missed day would turn into a missed week … and before long, it felt easier to drop out than to continue.

What could we do to help? We wondered if it might work better for moms if we had a weekly study that was topical rather than sequential and cumulative. If each week did not build upon the previous week, maybe mothers would feel better coming and going as life allowed. So in the fall of 2012, we piloted a class called Navigating Motherhood.

We started small, but for the first time our numbers stayed steady until the end of the semester. And in the spring of 2013, our numbers did not just hold, we grew. I began writing the curriculum for this study, and found out that I loved it. I had always enjoyed teaching and speaking on various topics, but never in my wildest dreams did I imagine that I would focus my speaking and writing on parenting. Even so, week after week, we could see the Lord's hand was on this. I believe we are close to the Lord's heart when we are encouraging those who are raising His children.

As semesters turned into years, our numbers continued to increase and hold. The tide of dwindling classes had finally changed. We came to see that mothers everywhere were looking for encouragement. If churches were willing to offer them the opportunity to receive it, they would come. I had the great honor of teaching the Navigating Motherhood class for seven years before passing the baton to others who share my heart for mothers and the Lord.

Most of what I know about parenting has been observed and experienced as a child of two parents who embraced the task wholeheartedly. I grew up in a great family. Both of my parents love the Lord and their four children. If I only gave you those three sentences, it would be a wonderful story, but you wouldn't know the depths of God's faithfulness. You see, my dad did not grow up in a home where the Lord was honored. In fact, it was quite the opposite. My dad had a difficult childhood and was raised in a home where alcohol was a constant presence.

It was my mom who introduced my dad to Jesus. They met at a stoplight when they were in high school. At the time, my dad drove a convertible, and my mom was with a friend who drove one, too. Their story gives testimony to a God who delights in the smallest details. They dated through college and were married. As my dad came to know Jesus better, he determined that he wanted a family that knew the blessing of God *and* the blessing of a godly father.

A Bible class teacher I had in high school used to say, "Jesus is in the statistics-busting business." Jesus certainly did that with my dad. Statistically, he should have been an alcoholic, abusive father, but because of Jesus, we never experienced any of that. In fact, we experienced a dad who was eager to encourage us at every turn. Jesus broke the chains that had held my dad's family of origin, and my dad walked away from those chains forever.

Regularly, I teach a class at Child Protective Services on motivation to change. As I look out at those faces, my heart swells. The room is filled with parents who love their children and are seeking a better path for their families. I love offering them the hope that one day, because of their decision, one of their children could stand before a crowd at CPS just like I do, sharing how the chains of violence or neglect have been broken in their family. Jesus has the ability to come into each of our lives and help us write a better story. I have lived it, and I have seen it.

And the best part?

Both of my dad's parents came to know Jesus later in life. The Lord transformed their lives, and they became two of the best grandparents out there.

My own parenting journey began in 1999 when I met and married Tony Brooks within seven months. I was overwhelmed with love for him right from the start. I remember waking up with a smile on my face before my mind was even clear enough to know why. My mind was still groggy with the morning, but my heart remembered Tony even in the deepest sleep. He was my person. To this day, walking down the aisle to him was the easiest thing I have ever done. All of our pictures of us leaving our ceremony are a bit blurry. We were *running* to start our new life together.

Our marriage has brought us joy, heartache, and growth. We each know Jesus better as a result of learning to love each other. We have four children: two sons, Payton and Benjamin, and two daughters, Eden and Shelby. At the time of this publication our boys are in high school, Eden is in middle school, and Shelby is in elementary. These four children share the same biology but have wildly different personalities. For a while I hoped that if we figured out how to be a great parent to one, we would have figured it out for all four. That was not to be. What worked in parenting Payton only served to frustrate Benjamin, and what brought about a desired response in Eden made Shelby stomp her foot and say, "No."

There isn't a parenting book out there that offers a one-size-fits-all method of parenting success. Jesus is the only One who has the keys to unlock the hearts of my children, and as my confidence in Him grew over the years, so did my confidence in mothering. I pray this book gives you a glimpse of what is possible for you, if you put your hope in the same One who holds me together..

I am still very much in the middle of my parenting journey, and I don't have all the answers. The fire that burns in my bones is encouraging moms, making sure they know that the Lord has created them to succeed and be blessed in motherhood. I want discouraged moms everywhere to know that Jesus is real and can be trusted. I want to point others to the God who saved me once for an eternity and has saved me again and again in the midst of mothering.

May I forever praise His name.

WHAT GOD HAS GIVEN YOU IN YOUR CHILDREN

Our children have always wanted a dog. We put them off for years, but one Christmas, in a moment of crazy, we purchased a much longed-for and prayed-for pup. Presenting our German Shepherd puppy to our children on Christmas morning is a sweet memory. They loved him instantly. For days, everyone fought over who got to take him out or fill his water dish. Whatever this dog needed, my children were ready.

A couple of weeks later, however, the newness had worn off. My husband and I wanted this dog to stay our children's responsibility so we started reminding them to meet his needs. It seemed that they had forgotten he had been their favorite Christmas gift.

We would say things like:

"Your *gift* needs food. Remember how excited you were to receive him?"
"Your *gift* needs to go outside."
"Who wants to take your *gift* on a walk?"

Our children would always groan, followed by a smile. They loved this dog. But, through our experience with him, I have learned one thing: It's harder to stay intentional with a gift when it starts requiring something of you.

As you look around your life today, what are the things you once received as a gift that now cause you to roll your eyes and groan? What has lost its joy because it now requires something of you? The Lord is eager to shift your perspective. The enemy of our hearts wants us to focus on the work. Our God wants us to remember the relationship, the love, the commitment, and the blessing that comes from continuously receiving a gift with a happy heart.

> *It's harder to stay intentional with a gift*
> *when it starts requiring something of you.*

Our children are now in the habit of caring for our dog. They love him and call his name as soon as they walk in the door. They feel his love, and what once felt like work brings them great joy again. They see him with fresh eyes, knowing that if the gift were gone, there would be an immediate ache in their lives.

May the Lord give you fresh eyes to see the gifts He has placed in your life, too.

YOU-ARE-HERE QUESTION

What is a gift that the enemy has been trying to make you view as a burden?

_____

_____

_____

Children are a gift from the Lord. That is a statement we would say we believe wholeheartedly. Yet, in the busy, hustle of "get your teeth brushed, let's figure out what you will eat for dinner, you need a diaper change, I forgot to pack a snack, I told you to go to the bathroom before we left the house, do you have a dirty diaper again, please give me my phone, how did you get a hole in those pants, I just mopped that floor, what do you mean you won't eat this" moments of motherhood, it is easy to lose sight of the gift.

The enemy works overtime to make sure we do. His full-time job is polluting the Lord's truth. He is the father of lies.

I'm sure you have never been more taken with humans than you are with your children. And at the same time, you are overwhelmed. Vision impaired. Tired. Scared. I am, too. At a time when we feel like we should be our best selves, we can start feeling as if we are at our worst. We can lose sight of who the Lord called us to be.

As we navigate motherhood, it is easy to focus on the constant energy required rather than on the gift we already have in our children. It is easy to miss the extravagance of what the Master has given.

In Matthew 25, Jesus tells us a parable that can minister to every mother. In it, He explains that a master called his servants together to tell them he was going away for a time and was entrusting them with some gold to steward in his absence.

One servant received five bags of gold, one received two bags, and another received one. Immediately, two of the servants invested their gifts, and the gifts grew. But the servant with one bag of gold did not want to take a risk, so he did not invest what he had been given. That servant was only concerned with "not losing" the gift.

When the master returned, that servant's gift was still the exact way it had been given. Nothing was lost, but that disappointed the master. He had trusted his servants with his treasure because he wanted them to experience his abundance. He had wanted growth. He had hoped they would see the value but not be paralyzed by it. The master was not looking for babysitters. He was looking for investors.

And He still is.

God's best gifts require something of us. There is great blessing in both the gift and the work it takes to receive it. The Lord has much bigger goals for us than just keeping our children safe. He hopes for so much more.

DROP-A-PIN VERSE

Children are a gift from the Lord; they are a reward from Him. Like arrows in the hand of a warrior are the children of one's youth. Blessed is the family who fill their quiver with them. They will not be put to shame when they speak with their enemies at the gate. Psalm 127:3 NLT

DIRECTION QUESTION

What could you do to show your appreciation for your gift?

_____

_____

_____

PRAYER PROMPT

Ask the Lord to expose the lies you have believed. Ask the Lord to restore to you the initial joy you felt in receiving your gift.

_____

_____

_____

Some mornings as I watch our boys walk into school, I'm overcome with emotion. In Scripture Jesus receives a particular blessing from His Father, and it is exactly what comes to mind in those moments. So I roll down the window and yell, "These are my sons, in whom I am well pleased!"

You can imagine what happens next.

My boys turn around, give the cutthroat sign, and break into a sprint. I'm convinced that's "boy-speak" for, "Mom, we're crazy about you, too."

It does my heart good to reflect on how the Father loved His Son. How he must have missed having Him around in heaven during His years on earth. There wasn't a moment of Jesus' earthly journey that His Father's eyes were not on Him. Yet in Matthew 3, the Father's love pours out in an intentional, audible blessing.

I know it comforted Jesus to hear His Father's voice.

I also know it blessed His Father to speak it.

YOU-ARE-HERE QUESTION

When was the last time you gave your child an intentional, audible blessing?

_____

_____

_____

When our children were young it was important to us that they learned to say "thank you." We wanted them to be polite, acknowledge generosity, and have a heart of gratitude.

My guess is our Father wants the same of His children.

Your children are a gift. When was the last time you thanked the Lord for them? How often do your kids hear you express appreciation out loud?

We have all felt that "mama bear instinct" rise up when our gift feels threatened or insulted. However, it has become culturally accepted to sit with friends and talk about how your children are driving you crazy …

And sometimes they are within earshot.

Have you ever noticed how many t-shirts and Internet memes insinuate that kids are enough to drive anyone to drink? Our little ones are seeing the same things we are. You see, Satan likes a two-for-one deal. I've already said he will work to convince you that God's gift is not a gift. And he will work twice as hard to convince your children of the same thing. Ask yourself, is there a chance your children could be internalizing the message that they are a burden?

You are going to have to watch your thought life here. Where do you go when you are losing your mind? Do you blame your child for everything? Imagine if you overheard your husband talking with his friends about how *you* were enough to drive him crazy or make him drink? You would be heartbroken. Yet it has been the norm for mothers to repeatedly insult their children in this manner.

We have forgotten they are a gift.

No one tells you that from the moment someone puts a child into your arms, it's "go time" … for the rest of your life. There is no question that raising children is stressful. Please do not hear me saying that motherhood is easy. We all have to learn a way to deal with the challenges. So only you can answer these questions:

1. What are your coping mechanisms?
2. Do they affirm your children?
3. Do they acknowledge they are a gift?

> *There is power in remembering the truth.*

We can plan ahead for the best ways to take a break. Sure, a trip to the day spa would be nice, but we need breaks more often than an occasional outing. I have learned my closet is my substitute day spa experience. I have a piece of paper on the wall in there that says, "Children are a gift." I go in there frequently to take a deep breath and read those words.

There is power in remembering the truth.

 ## DROP-A-PIN VERSE

Whoever receives one such child in my name, receives me, and whoever receives me, receives not me, but him who sent me.

Mark 9:37 ESV

DIRECTION QUESTION

Is it easy for you to remember that your child was made in the image of God? Why or why not?

_____

_____

_____

PRAYER PROMPT

Ask the Lord to remind you to intentionally and audibly bless your child. Ask Him to give you healthy coping mechanisms.

_____

_____

_____

One gorgeous spring day, the house was unusually quiet while my boys were at school, and my girls were both napping. Fresh air sounded good to me so I opened the door to our backyard, then walked over and sat down on our couch, expecting to have a moment of peace. All morning, I had been feeling drained by the constant demands of motherhood.

As I sat there, enjoying the stillness, my mind wandered to the Lord. I began to pray, and I asked Him to speak to my heart. As soon as I whispered, "Amen," a bird flew through the open door into our living room. I screamed in shock, which shocked the bird. He flew right into our ceiling fan. Thankfully, the fan did not seem to injure him, and he kept on flying around. And I don't know if it was the force of the fan or nature's call, but as the bird flew out of our living room, he relieved himself of an impressive amount of cargo all over our couch. Then, just like that, he flew out the back door and was gone. I sat there stunned, trying to take in what had just happened and wondering how I could clean up the mess and salvage our couch.

Then, I remembered the prayer I had just offered right before the bird had flown in.

Thinking of it, I laughed out loud. It is hard to explain, but in that moment of laughter, I deeply felt the Lord's presence. He was with me in the mayhem.

Sometimes life is wild. If we're not careful, we miss the hilarity in it because we're busy wondering what we can clean up and salvage. Be sure to look for joy in the mess. Don't miss the goodness of the Lord in the life you live.

Even in the middle of a mess, the Lord can be found.

And on the off chance you feel a little bit like that bird, enjoying a spring day when all of a sudden you fly though the wrong door and get hit hard by something unexpected ... keep going. God can redeem our wrong turns by allowing us to learn and lead others from our mistakes.

YOU-ARE-HERE QUESTION

When was the last time you laughed hard?

_____

_____

_____

Never forget that the enemy's goal is to pollute the gifts that God has given. Here are three ways to keep the blessing clear.

1. TAKE YOUR TIME. Make sure you are building a family schedule that you can live with, one that allows time to invest in your child. One of Satan's best tactics is to have each child and parent so ridiculously overscheduled that they are actually spending little to no time together. Sometimes you will need to get some fresh air and sit down. We can acknowledge that our children are gifts and still say that we have never had a more exhausting job. Being responsible for someone's life is overwhelming. It helps to acknowledge that we are human.

2. GIVE THANKS. Establish some new family habits that cause you to be thankful for your children in front of them. Sometimes at dinner our family will list things that make us smile, or as we are driving we will all list things that make us feel alive. By the way, while I was raised in a family that did all of these things growing up, my husband was not. I felt his eyebrows raise the first time I called out, "Everyone tell

me what you're thankful for! Backseat, you go first." This did not feel natural or normal to him at all, but he did it. Now, years later, our teenagers raise their eyebrows, but everyone participates. We wanted a family who knew how to be thankful. That was going to take practice. Thanksgiving is not just a holiday, it's a way of life.

> *Thanksgiving is not just a holiday,*
> *it's a way of life.*

3. REFRAME. Stress will come. There may be a way to reframe it as a blessing. For instance, our laundry drives me nuts. It feels like I could be doing laundry 24 hours a day and never catch up. I can just see the mound of clothes in front of our washer and feel my neck get tight with stress. So I have formed the habit of saying in that moment, "Praise God for healthy kids who have the ability to change clothes." Remembering that there is a gift at the root of my stress helps me keep things in perspective.

 ## DROP-A-PIN VERSE

He settles the childless woman in her home as a happy mother of children. Praise the LORD.   Psalm 113:9

DIRECTION QUESTION

Where have you experienced joy as a parent?

_____

_____

_____

PRAYER PROMPT

Ask the Lord to remind you of the fun you have had in being a mother. Ask Him for more opportunities to laugh with your family.

_____

_____

_____

Eden: Mom, are you confident in God, even when your prayers aren't answered the way you want?"

Me: That's faith. It's trusting in Him, even when I don't understand. But I keep talking to Him, asking Him to remind me that He is enough. Often, He changes my heart instead of my circumstances.

Eden: The hardest part is seeing other people get what I want and trusting that He's heard me. I know He loves me even when I'm not getting what I know He could give.

Me (*suddenly feeling moved and teary*): Yes. Eden, can you tell me what you're asking Him for? I'd love to be praying with you.

Eden: An Elf on the Shelf.

And just like that, my tears were gone. Sweet girl. Her definition of a heartfelt desire doesn't always match mine.

YOU-ARE-HERE QUESTION

What request do you see your children bringing to you in abundance?

_____

_____

_____

I am thankful for the opportunity to hear any of my children express what is on their heart. It doesn't mean Tony and I are always going to get it for them, but there's a sweetness in knowing what our children desire. They are our treasure. Yet, we have to remember that before they were ours, they were His. They are "God's Home Improvement Loan" to us.

The Lord is writing an individual story in each of us and in each of our children. Everyone has their own story, and with that comes unique interests and desires. Your child's story is not going to look exactly like yours. Trust that the Lord is writing one that is wonderfully creative and different in both you and your children. Remember that your children cannot carry your self-esteem. They are going to make mistakes, and they are going to need a mom who can see past herself to see what Jesus is doing.

> *Remember that your children*
> *cannot carry your self-esteem.*

Jesus offers a bridge back to relationship; you can be a mom who offers one as well. You and your child may not always see eye-to-eye, and that can leave you feeling alone. The Lord is longing to collaborate with you in this process. Please don't think you are doing this on your own. God knew what He was doing when He placed your child in your home, and He knew there would be times when you don't agree. Somehow, in His goodness, His intention is to grow you and your child to look more like Jesus ... with and because of *each other*.

 ## DROP-A-PIN VERSE

For this child I prayed, and the Lord has granted me my petition that I made him. Therefore I have lent him to the Lord. As long as he lives, he is lent to the Lord.   1 Samuel 1:27-28 NLT

DIRECTION QUESTION

How do you plan to encourage your child with the news that the Lord loves them, even when they don't get what they want?

_____

_____

_____

PRAYER PROMPT

Ask the Lord to help you trust the story he is writing in you and in the life of your child.

_____

_____

_____

Years ago, a friend and I spent the day scouting locations for our church's annual women's conference. My mom had helped me by keeping Eden while I was away. At the end of the day, my friend and I met my mom at a coffee shop to pick up Eden.

I thanked my mom, buckled Eden in her seat, we said our quick goodbyes, and left the parking lot. We had been driving in end-of-day traffic for about five minutes when I noticed something moving fast in my peripheral vision. A truck drove through the shrubs that lined the street, and entered the street, perpendicular to oncoming traffic.

We were already moving at a steady speed, and I knew the truck would not hit us, but I will never forget the sound of that truck hitting the car directly behind us. I glanced into my rearview mirror, and saw an explosion of dust and shattered glass.

Stunned, I whispered to my friend, "I think we just saw someone get killed."

The truck had broadsided a Suburban then crashed through the wall of a bank. The cab of the truck landed in the middle of someone's office. The Suburban it had hit had spun off the road and directly into a telephone pole. Naturally, I slowed down to see what we needed to do.

It's amazing how fast your mind works in situations like these. In a fraction of a second, I thought I recognized the Suburban, but wasn't sure. I asked my friend, "Was my mom behind us?"

She said, "No, she was going to meet your dad ..."

But before she finished her sentence, we both realized that the Suburban behind us was my mom's. I'll never forget the sound of both of our voices as we both began crying out, "Jesus. Jesus. Jesus ..."

We cried out to our Savior, and we didn't stop. We were still saying His name as I pulled over and ran to my mom's car, where she was slumped over her steering wheel, but she was breathing.

An ambulance took my mom to the hospital, and the man who'd been driving the truck went by helicopter. We were thrilled when both were treated and released that night with minor injuries. Miraculously no one at the bank had been injured.

At the time of the accident, one of my brothers was living out of state. I called him that night to go over the events of the day and give him an update on our mother. As the shock of the moment wore off, and I was able to think through things, I told my brother, "I have been praying all my life. I know how to bring someone before the Lord. Yet at the moment mom needed me most, all I could do was say the name of Jesus."

My brother is wise, and he quickly responded, "Don't feel anything but great about that. In whispering the name of Jesus you summoned all the power that is to be had. I think that was the most powerful prayer you have ever prayed."

It's not just that Jesus saves our souls. He also saves our days.

I think about that conversation a lot. There are so many times as a mother that I don't know what to say, so I try that powerful prayer again. I whisper the name of Jesus. His name is connected to His power. Being able to say His name and access His power is the best thing the Lord has ever given us. It's not just that Jesus saves our souls. He also saves our days.

Are you struggling to remember your children are a gift? Say His name. He is ready to help you remember.

YOU-ARE-HERE QUESTION

Is there a situation where you need to whisper the name of Jesus?

_____

_____

_____

The accident with my mom taught me how quickly life can change. The people and things we take for granted today will not be with us forever. There has never been a better time to treat our children as a gift. Here are a few helpful tips that I continually try.

- Smile.
- Be your children's fan.
- Encourage at every turn.
- Truly believe in them.
- Put people to bed on time (especially yourself).
- Be aware of how long you are letting your children have screen time.
- Watch for signs that your children and/or their parents need to slow down.
- Do not let "FOMO" (Fear Of Missing Out) with your friends cause you to miss out with your child.
- Discipline your children. You will always love them, but are you raising them so that other people will?
- Say you are sorry. You are going to make mistakes. Apologize.
- Do not put their failures out for public consumption on social media
- Don't forget that the Lord intended for some of this to be fun!

- Slow down to listen to your child laugh. Commit to making sure you do that at least once a day.
- Do not forget who you are or what type of mother you want to be.
- Go ahead and work the puzzle.
- Go ahead and play the game.
- Let the house be dirty for a while.
- Have a day where you concentrate more on saying yes than no.
- Get a list of free activities and do a few of them.
- Remember that you serve a patient God.

 ## DROP-A-PIN VERSE

May the Lord give you increase more and more, you and your children! May you be blessed by the Lord who made the heaven and the earth. Psalm 115:14-15 NLT

DIRECTION QUESTION

Which bullet point on the list do you want to focus on this week?

_____

_____

_____

PRAYER PROMPT

You already know your children are a gift. Ask the Lord to help you *feel* it today.

_____

_____

_____

WHEN YOU
NEED GRACE

I made a mistake yesterday. A huge mistake. The kind of mistake that makes your body shake with adrenaline.

We have had a stomach virus at our house this week, and it has made for many a sleepless night. Unfortunately, our son Benjamin hallucinates when he gets a fever. Throughout the night his fever comes and goes, and so do his nightmares and confusion. He cries, saying he doesn't know me, that he wants his mother, that he misses his dad.

It's heartbreaking. And tiring. We have not slept much.

The other night his temperature rose as he slept. Then he woke and started to cry, talking of being all alone.

Again and again, I assured him he was *not* alone, but he couldn't understand. He stayed sad and confused, until I said, "Son, do you remember who Jesus is?"

"Yes, He is the Son of God."

"Can you tell me *where* He is?"

"Yes, He is right here."

Just saying Jesus' name and acknowledging His presence brought peace and clarity to both of us. It was a sweet moment during the kind of week that sweet moments can be lost and forgotten. Somewhere, I lost track of days.

Monday, Tuesday, and Wednesday went by like a whirlwind, and I didn't even realize it was Thursday until Tony said, "Shouldn't Shelby be in school on Thursdays?"

"Oh, no! I forgot ..." I said, realizing. Yes, I had forgotten to take Shelby to school, but had I forgotten anything else? I didn't stop to ask myself.

Later that morning, I was helping Benjamin take a breathing treatment, surveying a house in desperate need of disinfectant, thinking I should take a much-needed shower, and wondering where to get started on it all when I received a text from a number I didn't recognize.

Let me know when you are close.

I looked at the text for a few seconds, but nothing came to mind. Then I looked at a clock and realized I was supposed to be speaking to a group of moms at that very minute.

"Lord, have mercy," I whispered.

And He did. I was presentable in two-and-a-half minutes. Thankfully, the previous weekend, I had gone over my notes and marked my Bible so I was prepared. On top of that, I knew exactly where everything was. Then I was on the road with a sick child that I was able to place in the care of a nearby family member. And all of it happened in just a few minutes. From beginning to end, it was a miracle.

As I drove to the event, I berated myself for making such a colossal error. Then I felt the Spirit remind me of that sweet moment with Benjamin from earlier in the week.

He asked, "Do you remember who Jesus is?"

My heart responded, "He is the Son of God, and He is right here." Truth settled my soul.

Only a few minutes later, I stood up in front of a group of moms to speak about how our God is glorified in weakness and how He takes what we have and multiplies it to bless others. As I spoke, I knew I was experiencing a loaves-and-fish moment myself. I had given Him what I had—which did not appear to be much—and He had fed a room full of people. Before my eyes, I saw a group of moms nourished by the truth that God has equipped them for this job of motherhood. I saw them take courage. On top of it all, I felt them encourage me. As they extended me grace, I saw our God, who so readily extends grace to each of us. In spite of my hectic morning, that message represented one of my better moments.

So how does one of your worst moments become one of your best?

You give it to Jesus. He's there, right beside you, ready to cover you in grace. You have not caught Him off guard. He is not surprised by your imperfections. He is ready to reveal His glory.

Give Him what you have, even if it is only a little. He is a miracle worker. I saw it with my own eyes.

YOU-ARE-HERE QUESTION

In what ways are you questioning yourself as a mother?

With so many questions on our minds, how do we find peace in the midst of motherhood? Peace is only found when we trust Jesus.

He is the answer.

But we have an enemy who wants us to keep questioning. He wants to take our flaws and use them as a wedge between us and the Lord. Actually, he wants to use them as a wedge between us and *everyone*.

Isolation is his goal for you. He wants you to feel alone, abandoned, and unloved. And he wants you to believe you are the only one who feels that way. Jesus, however, reminds us in Matthew 9:12-13, "Healthy people don't need to see a doctor, but the sick will go for treatment ... I have come to invite the outcasts of society and sinners, not those who think they are already on the right path" (TPT).

Jesus came for you *before* you were healthy. He came for you in your weakness. He is with you in the midst of your mistakes.

In my life, I can so quickly focus on all the areas where I do not measure up:

- I wish I were better at planning birthday parties for my children.
- I wish my car were cleaner.
- I wish my body looked different.
- I wish I were more organized.
- I wish I were kinder.
- I wish I did not raise my voice so easily.

My list could go on and on. If I am not careful, I allow my list to drive me away from the Lord and others. My list of shortcomings can make me want to hide. But I don't have to clean myself up in order to come to Him. He wants me just as I am.

> When He gave your children
> to you, He knew they would bring out the
> very best **and** the very worst in you.

That's the way He wants you, too. Just as you are. Your children might have been a surprise to you, but they were no surprise to God. When He gave your children to you, He knew they would bring out the very best and the very worst in you. He already knew you would feel overwhelmed at times so He made a way for you to find peace.

DROP-A-PIN VERSE

Are you tired? Worn out? Burned out on religion? Come to me. Get away with me and you'll recover your life. I'll show you how to take a real rest. Walk with me and work with me—watch how I do it. Learn the unforced rhythms of grace. I won't lay anything heavy or ill-fitting on you. Keep company with me and you'll learn to live freely and lightly. Matthew 11:28-30 (MSG)

DIRECTION QUESTION

What about this verse is comforting to you as you face the future?

_____

_____

_____

PRAYER PROMPT

Spend some time asking the Lord to help you take hold of this invitation in a new way. Tell Him about the areas where you are struggling. Tell Him where you are feeling confident. Tell Him that you want to navigate motherhood with Him at your side.

_____

_____

_____

Recently, Tony and I got into one of the biggest arguments we have had in years. It started when he said something that was incredibly offensive to me. In the moment, I felt like I had never been more insulted, more unappreciated, more hurt. His words brought immediate tears and a strong response from me.

Wondering what he said?

It went something like this: "Do you mind shutting the laundry room door when the dryer is going?"

Full disclosure: You should know, Tony never really joined in my argument. I think he was completely astonished by the response he received. He had not spoken in a harsh or sarcastic tone; he had simply asked a question.

You should also know, he asked this question while we were on Round Two with the stomach bug. Hence, the reason the dryer was going at 6 a.m. Tony had been helpful throughout our week of sickness, but this mom was exhausted and completely spent. Have you ever felt tired enough to almost forget who you are?

Last Friday morning, I was there.

Once, I taught a lesson I called *Love is Patient, Love is Kind ... Love is Really, Really Tired.* These days with young children are some of the best days of my life. But the best days of my life sometimes bring out the worst parts of me.

YOU-ARE-HERE QUESTION

Has there been a time when the best days of your life brought out the worst in you?

_____

_____

_____

So, what can we do when the best of times are also the worst of times?

First, apologize. The enemy often tries to hit me with guilt when I have made a mistake. I've learned to watch for that. I don't want to be stuck feeling bad about an area where God can be praised, and He is helping me move forward. Satan may have momentary victories, but Jesus is the One who wins it all. When I apologize to someone I have wronged—and even when I forgive someone who has wronged me—it is one way Jesus moves me forward.

> *Satan may have momentary victories, but*
> *Jesus is the One who wins it all.*

Next, recognize that sometimes the best thing we can do for God's Kingdom (and our families) is go to bed. Ignore the to-do list and take a nap. And what if you can't? I find myself praying Psalm 127:2 often: "The Lord grants sleep to those He loves." The key word is *grant*. I know He loves me, and there are days when I cannot stop and rest, so I ask Him to grant me sleep in the same way He grants me peace ... supernaturally.

Finally, recognize the joy in your situation. Gratitude is energizing. Thankfulness plugs the drain that threatens to empty us of Living Water. Hard days come and go. Sometimes, those hard days turn into hard weeks, hard months, and hard years. So anchor yourself to something that holds. God's Word holds. Find a verse and put it on repeat in your mind. For years, I have held on to, "Because of the Lord's great love we are not consumed, for His compassions never fail. They are new every morning; great is your faithfulness. I say to myself, 'The Lord is my portion; therefore I will wait for Him'" Lamentations 3:22-24.

Sure, there are days when I *feel* consumed, but I am anchored to a God who can't be. That truth allows me to sway with the wind instead of break. And on the days I do break, that truth brings me back to who our God is. He hasn't asked for perfection. He offers me grace upon grace.

It is good to remember that God has set this work before me. Even in the middle of the night, God is leading me in the ministry of motherhood.

This morning at 3 a.m. I was summoned to Round Three of the stomach bug hitting our family. I was doing laundry by 3:30 AM.

But this time a fresh perspective changed everything. With a tired smile, I shut the door on the way out.

 DROP-A-PIN VERSE

May the favor of the Lord our God rest on us: establish the work of our hands for us—yes, establish the work of our hands.

Psalm 90:17

DIRECTION QUESTION

Where in your life do you need a fresh perspective on the ministry of motherhood today?

_____

_____

_____

PRAYER PROMPT

Ask the Lord what work He is establishing in your life. Ask Him for grace for the task at hand. Then lean into His favor.

_____

_____

_____

Setting: *Family breakfast table*
Characters: *All four kids eating, while mom unloads dishwasher*

Eden: The Lord really does hear our prayers.

(No acknowledgment from her siblings)

Eden: Do you all remember last night on the way to church when Mom was a little bit losing her mind?

(Brothers both raise their heads and nod, Shelby drops her blanket and nods. Mom realizes it must have been more impressive than she thought.)

Eden: Well, during prayer requests at church, I asked my teachers and my friends to please pray for my mom. And they did. And now she's back to smiling. She's our kind and sweet mom again. She's not even a little bit crazy.

Sweet mercy. God is good. Even in my flaws He can reveal Himself. He takes parenting fails and turns them into wins.

His strength, not mine.

His power, not mine.

His grace, not mine.

His goodness, not mine.

He lets His testimony become … mine.

Confidence that is centered on needing Jesus allows us to admit the weakness that our culture would encourage us to hide. At one point in my life, my face would have flushed at the thought of my daughter asking her Bible class to pray for her "crazy mom," but the Lord is teaching me that we all need grace. I am starting to see the beauty in asking for it.

My brother once asked me, "What is something you do really well in parenting?"

Thinking a while, I answered, "I think my kids would say I'm best at needing Jesus."

Jesus is the only One who has it all together.

I suppose it would be nice to be known for my baked goods, my pristine home, or never getting upset when my children can't find their shoes, but none of those things are my claim to fame. My claim is: "I need Jesus a lot."

Jesus is the only One who has it all together.

YOU-ARE-HERE QUESTION

Where are you most tempted to act as if you have it all together?

_____

_____

_____

I want to be a mom who daily reminds myself that my confidence is in Christ alone. Remember, our children were never meant to carry our self-esteem. No one but Jesus can sustain that weight. So we look to grow in our confidence.

We remember that our confidence in Christ:

- Allows us to be bold in Jesus' name.
- Sets us apart.
- Allows us to admit to others that we don't know what we are doing.

- Teaches us to place our trust in God to bring about His good in spite of our weakness.
- Causes us to seek the Lord in deeper ways because we acknowledge how dependent we are on Him.

Grace infuses our everyday parenting with hope. Jesus comes in and reminds us that our actions and performance have no bearing on His great love for each of us. Jesus is the only One who has ever lived this earthly life perfectly. He did this to free us from the burden of perfection. He sets us free to experience grace.

When we take hold of grace, we take hold of something that is counterculture. The world we live in is all about producing results. Yet, because of Jesus, our confidence is no longer performance-based. Our self esteem no longer comes from how well our baby is nursing or how they are sleeping through the night. We realize whether our toddler is the first to sing the ABCs or the first to bite someone in the nursery, Jesus is the basis for who we are. It's all grace. He is the foundation of our mothering and He doesn't change.

DROP-A-PIN VERSE

Each time he said, "My grace is all you need. My power works best in weakness.' So now I am glad to boast about my weaknesses, so that the power of Christ can work through me. That's why I take pleasure in my weaknesses, and in the insults, hardships, persecutions, and troubles that I suffer for Christ. For when I am weak, then I am strong.   2 Corinthians 12:9-11 NLT

DIRECTION QUESTION

Where do you want to take hold of God's grace in your weakness?

_____

_____

_____

PRAYER PROMPT

Ask the Lord for His increasing strength to be displayed in your mothering.

_____

_____

_____

When my boys were toddlers, getting them loaded into the car sometimes felt as if I were trying to put a wild animal in a four-point harness. Without fail, I would buckle one of them in and move to get the next one buckled ... only to have the first one unbuckle himself and commence hopping through our car like a spider monkey. I remember one day I completely lost my mind. I yelled at both of my boys. I can still hear my raised voice telling them I was done with them, when I looked up and saw a family from church walking by.

My face flushed red as I tried to change into a sweeter voice, "Why, hello Angela! How good to see you."

I could hear the "fake" in my voice, and I knew the other mom could hear it as well. I still wonder why I didn't just look at her and honestly say, "It's a hard day in the Brooks family."

The shame I felt as I drove away that day followed me around like a black cloud.

I was not raised by a family who yelled. Yet two toddlers into motherhood, I realized that I had become a yeller. I didn't want to be that way, but I also knew I had to figure a way to "baby step" myself out of a bad habit.

Our children had been listening to me pray since birth so they immediately bowed their heads every time they heard the Lord's name. That helped me devise a plan. Rather than yelling at my children, I started praying loud.

"LORD, HELP ME LOVE THESE BOYS WHEN THEY BOTH KNOW THEY ARE NOT SUPPOSED TO BE STANDING ON THE KITCHEN TABLE."

"LORD, GIVE ME STRENGTH WHEN MY CHILDREN MANAGE TO TAKE OFF THEIR CLOTHES OR SHOES WHILE IN THEIR CAR SEAT."

Although this practice seems ridiculous as I write about it now, I have to admit, it got our boys' attention. As soon as they heard the Lord's name, they would each bow their heads. Even better, as I prayed, the Lord would allow me to see that He was working on me, just as he was working on my sons.

YOU-ARE-HERE QUESTION

Is there something in your mothering, a bad habit or tendency, that follows you?

_____

_____

_____

I still yell sometimes, but it's not who I am as a mother. The Lord doesn't taunt me with my past mistakes.

My flaws don't have to be a dark cloud that follows me everywhere.

Based on Romans 8:1 we can claim, "Those who enter into Christ's being here for us no longer have to live under a continuous, low-lying black cloud. A new power is in operation. The Spirit of life in Christ, like a strong wind, has magnificently cleared the air, freeing you from a fated lifetime of brutal tyranny at the hands of sin and death" (MSG).

Sin will always separate us from God, but Jesus has cleared the way. Knowing that grace removes the cloud, we can begin to decipher when we are hearing from the Lord or when we are hearing from the enemy.

> *The Lord has made a way for you*
> *to come through the cloud with confidence*
> *and bring Him your needs.*

The Lord brings conviction and the desire to change.

The enemy brings guilt and paralysis.

The Lord works in the light. Satan works in the black cloud. He wants to make you think that you should be able to do this on your own. If you believe that long enough you will think *you* are the black cloud.

But that is not who you are.

The Lord has made a way for you to come through the cloud with confidence and bring Him your needs.

 DROP-A-PIN VERSE

Let us approach the throne of grace with confidence, so that we may receive mercy and find grace to help us in our time of need.

Hebrews 4:16

DIRECTION QUESTION

What do you sense the Lord saying to you right now about the cloud that has been blocking your vision of who you can be as a mother?

_____

_____

_____

PRAYER PROMPT

Confidently ask Him for what you and your family needs today.

_____

_____

_____

Do you remember the innocent days before you were a mother? Does it make you laugh to think of the things you used to promise yourself you would never do?

I remember a sweet friend bringing us dinner after we had just had our first baby. While she was at our house, she lay her toddler down on the floor of our living room and changed his dirty diaper.

I was mortified! Instantly, I was full of judgment.

After she left, I said to Tony, "I will never change a dirty diaper where someone else can see. How disgusting."

I smile when I tell this story now. Four children later, I have changed many diapers in public. When toddlers need to be changed, they need to be changed. I have lost my ability to judge because I have now walked in the shoes of my friend.

It's so easy as mothers to feel contempt for people who do not parent the same way we parent. We have to remember that The Lord is writing a unique story in each mother. Grace allows us to open our arms wide to the people around us because we realize we need grace just as much as they do. When we see how flawed we are, we have no time to let flaws become a barrier between others and us.

YOU-ARE-HERE QUESTION

Have you ever felt judged as a mother?

_____

_____

_____

Our Lord's love is never ending. And if we tap into Him, ours can be never ending, as well. When there is a limitless supply of something, you don't worry about running out. You can smile. You can bless. You can encourage. You can give. You can celebrate. You can donate. You can hug. You can trust. You can be hurt. You can recover. You can feel deeply. You can grieve. You can hope. You can know in your heart of hearts that the God who created the universe is with you, and He is enough for you.

His grace covers everything.

Our Lord's love is never ending. And if we tap into Him, ours can be never ending, as well.

Part of accepting grace from God is extending it to others. When we acknowledge our imperfections, walls come down. Satan wants you to think that you are bricked in by your failures or guilt. In truth, they are only paper walls, easily punched through by speaking them out loud.

Moms have a tendency to get the word out when something works great for us. A great pediatrician—*Share the news!* Free kids meals—*You should try it!* A better sleep method for newborns—*Lay it on me!*

Our social media posts are filled with nuggets of wisdom we want to share with other mothers. So how about this one:

Jesus has set us free from judgment.

Let's find a way to acknowledge the incredible news. We have been set free from judging and set free from being judged. That is the best news ever. Get the word out to your friends.

DROP-A-PIN VERSE

Now God has us where he wants us, with all the time in this world and the next to shower grace and kindness upon us in Christ Jesus. Saving is all his idea, and all his work. All we do is trust him enough to let him do it. It's God's gift from start to finish. We don't play a major role. If we did, we'd probably go around bragging that we had done the whole thing. No, we neither make nor save ourselves. God does both the making and the saving. He creates each of us by Christ Jesus to join him in the work he does, the good work he has gotten ready for us to do, work we had better be doing.   Ephesians 2:8 MSG

DIRECTION QUESTION

What area of your life do you want to look different this week because you know our God's supply of love is never ending?

_____

_____

_____

PRAYER PROMPT

If there is another mother that you have been judging, take a moment to confess and then pray that she would feel the Lord's lavish grace.

_____

_____

_____

WHEN YOUR CHILD STRUGGLES

When I was pregnant with Payton, I remember one morning I called my mom about 2 AM in a full panic. I had just read that our baby was the size of a piece of rice, and there was so much important development taking place.

"What if something goes wrong?" I cried.

My mom, rather calmly for 2 a.m., said, "When we hang up, I want you to get down on your knees and give this baby to the Lord. Tell the Lord you trust Him with this child. It won't be the last time you do it. Start doing this now, because that piece of rice is going to grow and grow. Surrendering that life to the Lord is going to get harder and harder. You will be thankful you've been practicing surrendering all along."

I learned an important truth that night. First, when I was struggling, my mother did not offer me false comfort or hope. She pointed me to the Lord and steered me toward surrender. So often we want to pull our children out of the struggle, but as parents, that is not our job. Our job is to point our children to the Lord.

My mom was right. My baby *has* grown, and these days, he's more man than child. So last night, when fear woke me up again, I got up and did what my mom taught me many years ago ...

I got down on my knees.

The enemy would love for me to be gripped by fear, but the truth is, when I'm wide awake I can acknowledge I'm gripped by love. My love for Payton woke me up. It was waking me up long before he drew his first breath. I've shed some tears, wishing I could protect him from every pain. But I'm asking the Lord to take each tear and receive it as gratitude for what He has given me. The opportunity to love is a gift I cherish. The discomfort of seeing our children struggle reveals the depths of our love.

> *The discomfort of seeing our children struggle*
> *reveals the depths of our love.*

Tony tells me about a time his mom hesitated to let him go on a trip with his youth group. He said she was nervous something would happen to him. I can understand that. As a mother, we most always feel our children are safest when they are with us.

But Tony's response is something that can increase the courage in all of us. "Something did happen each time she let me go. I grew."

YOU-ARE-HERE QUESTION

Is there an area where you find it difficult to let your child grow?

_____

_____

_____

When the Lord created our children, He could have made them perfect. Instead, each of our children have built-in challenges, part of their personalities that they will need to overcome. Every challenge is an opportunity. There will always be difficult people, teachers, friends, and family in their lives. On top of that, there may be sickness, disability, learning differences, character issues, and more "opportunities to overcome."

As a parent, your God-given instinct is to protect, and as far as safety is concerned, yes, you should. But there is another

God-given gift as well, and that is to allow your child to grow through struggle. We want to be training ourselves that in tough and wonderful moments, our first response is always to look to the Lord. He knows the path you take. He also knows the path for your child.

Some struggles are man-made, while some are God-given. Some are the result of a fallen world. When we have the perspective that *any* struggle can be used by God to push us and our children closer to Him, we realize what our response should be.

We walk by faith, no matter the path.

Psalm 139:7-10 tells us, "I can never be lost to your Spirit! I can never get away from my God. If I go up to heaven, you are there; if I go down to the place of the dead, you are there. If I ride the morning wind to the farthest oceans, even there your hand will guide me. Your strength will support me" (TLB).

You are never alone.

The enemy will use pain to make you think you have been abandoned. It's a lie. We know:

1. The Lord loves us.
2. The Lord has made a way for us.
3. The Lord is for us.

And so we learn to trust Him more, asking Him how to lead our children through struggle in a way that helps them grow closer to God rather than away from Him. We ask for His perspective, wisdom, and the supernatural ability to put courage into our children through our words and actions.

DROP-A-PIN VERSE

So do not fear, for I am with you;
   do not be dismayed, for I am your God.
I will strengthen you and help you;
   I will uphold you with my righteous right hand.

Isaiah 41:10

DIRECTION QUESTION

What can you do to support your child in order that they might grow through struggle?

_____

_____

_____

PRAYER PROMPT

Ask The Lord to help you when your child's ache blurs your vision. Ask Him to strengthen your confidence in His ability to work in all things.

_____

_____

_____

Every once in a while our family will go out to eat at a nice restaurant. And when I say nice, I mean a place where you have to tip someone who is actually serving you.

To understand this story, it is important that you understand the breakdown of the Brooks family. There are six of us, and we are split evenly down the middle as three extroverts and three introverts.

Team Introvert prefers that when we walk into a restaurant, we go straight to our seats and get focused on the task at hand: ordering our food. Tony leads Team Introvert.

I lead Team Extrovert. Team Extrovert has a tendency to walk into a restaurant and immediately start looking around to see if we know anyone there. We enjoy waving and smiling at people we know and even those that we don't. Sometimes this trait makes Team Introvert uncomfortable. On this particular day I remember thinking that Team Extrovert had done a good job of not drawing attention to ourselves upon entering the restaurant.

As we sat down, I remember noticing how cute Tony was in his navy blue pullover and glasses. Everyone then started looking at their menus except for 10-year-old Eden who, unbeknownst to us, started building a stack of small, plastic half-and-half containers on her corner of the table. Suddenly, she made a fist and slammed it down on the stack. It was a shock to all of us, especially because she is on Team Introvert.

In fact, because she is an introvert, Eden was mortified at the commotion that ensued. Five half-and-half containers exploding made a loud enough noise that the whole restaurant got quiet to see what was happening.

You might think that cream would have splattered everywhere but it didn't. The full blast all went one direction.

On Tony.

The majority of the table was unaffected. Tony, however, was coated in cream. Here Tony was, in the middle of the restaurant, with all eyes on him, as he slowly removed his glasses to clean them. All of us waited for the reaction we knew was coming. Yet, no reaction came. Tony, put his glasses back on, looked at Eden and said in a calm tone, "Don't ever do that again."

Then he wiped off his sweater and went back to looking at his menu.

One of our boys, who was still taking in the scene, said, "Dad, what happened to you? Where's your huge reaction. Usually things like this make you so mad."

Tony's response has stayed with us all. He said, "I don't like that I am someone who has huge reactions. I feel bad every time I act like that. I have been asking the Lord to change me, and I believe He is doing it."

It was a moment that captured the power of God at work in Tony's life. Our children know our struggles well. When we give them the opportunity to see the Lord change those flaws by His power, they come to know our God better and trust Him more.

YOU-ARE-HERE QUESTION

Is there an area of your life where you are tempted to say, "That's just who I am?" Could it be an area where the Lord may be wanting you to change?

_____

_____

_____

We all have a testimony. Our testimony is the story that shows how the Lord works in our lives. And our children have the opportunity to see that story lived out in real time right before their eyes. That means that as you parent, your children see up close that faith makes a difference or that faith is just something you talk about.

Our children have a front row seat to our victories and our struggles. Our actions either point to us believing in prayer, or they point to the fact that we don't. This is in no way a call to perfection; it is a call to honest living before your children. You do not have to do everything right, but you do have to remember you serve a Savior you can rely on. Your consistency in admitting and living out your need for Jesus is vital. Your children want to see that you carry your sadness, your doubt, your hopes, and your dreams straight to Jesus. Jesus can be your first response in victory and in loss so that your children learn He can be their first response as well.

Our testimony grows stronger through the deliverance of the Lord, and our children grow stronger as well.

When I feel as if I have failed royally as a parent, I often remind myself that my failing, placed in the hands of God, might actually be some of my best work. It is easy to model for our children how to handle success. It's even enjoyable. But the hard work comes in modeling failing, in admitting to our children, "I do not like how this turned out in my life, and I want it to be different. Would you pray with me that the Lord will show me a new way?"

Because we know God, we know He has the ability to bring value from anything. In a transaction only the Lord could bring about, He often turns pain into power. Because we have fallen and gotten up, our confidence and assurance in the Lord grows. And our children gain some of that same confidence and assurance just by watching it take place. Our testimony grows stronger through the deliverance of the Lord, and our children grow stronger as well.

DROP-A-PIN VERSE

And they triumphed over him by the blood of the Lamb and the word of their testimony ... Revelation 12:11

DIRECTION QUESTION

Can you think of a time the Lord has helped you overcome? How at ease are you in sharing this story with your children?

PRAYER PROMPT

Ask the Lord to help you and your family rely on Him. Ask Him to give you opportunities to talk about God's great power at work in your life.

DAY 3

I remember struggling in 5th grade and begging my parents to let me move schools. One day my mom came up to the school and got me out of class, and I was filled with hope that she and my dad were making a change for me. I cried when we didn't leave campus. I begged her to take me home or anywhere else. Instead, we went outside of the building and talked. Then she prayed that God would give me eyes to see the friends that I might be overlooking. She prayed that I would never miss any gift He was willing to give me.

I went back into the school feeling more irritated than blessed.

Her prayers weren't answered overnight, but you know who was in that 5th grade classroom? One of my very best friends, who has now stood by me during the best and hardest moments of my life. If I had gotten what I wanted and moved to another school, I would have missed that friendship and so much more.

My parents held me during that rough season of loneliness. They never left my side. They did not move me out of discomfort but allowed the Lord to work in it. He used that season for me. Through my sadness the Lord was laying a foundation for character and trust to develop.

YOU-ARE-HERE QUESTION

Have you ever experienced the Lord bringing something of value from something that was painful?

_____

_____

_____

Our instincts as mothers cause us to immediately try to stop tears when they start. A baby cries, and we rush to make it stop. An elementary student comes home upset, and we want names and a teacher to email. The angst of watching a teen navigate through the world of social media is enough to make a mother want to break every cell phone that ever existed (or is that just me?). Anything that causes our children pain, we want to fast-track out of their lives. Yet, pain is part of the growth process. And we want our children to grow.

> *Troubles will come, but so will*
> *our overcoming Savior.*

When my children are hurting, I don't want to become focused on stopping the pain. Lately, I am having to ask God to give me a bigger vision. I want growth in my children and in myself. Trouble is often part of that process. But trouble won't be the only thing we see. We will also see our Savior revealed. In John 16:33 Jesus says, "I have told you these things, so that in me you may have peace. In this world you will have trouble. But take heart! I have overcome the world."

The enemy will work to convince you that pain means something has gone wrong, but Jesus tells us something different. Troubles will come, but so will our overcoming Savior.

May we constantly be asking God to give us His vision for our children. He loves us and loves our children, yet He tells us in His Word, "We also glory in our sufferings, because we know that suffering produces perseverance; perseverance, character; and character, hope. And hope does not put us to shame, because God's love has been poured out into our hearts through the Holy Spirit that has been given to us" (Romans 5:3-5).

Most of the time, we want what God has to offer, yet we want to avoid the suffering. If we try to smooth every path we do so to the detriment of our children. There will be times when your child needs an advocate in you, but there will be many more times that what they actually need is you beside them whispering, "This is hard, but we've got this."

 DROP-A-PIN VERSE

But blessed is the one who trusts in the Lord, whose confidence is in him. They will be like a tree planted by the water that sends out its roots to the stream. It does not fear when heat comes; its leaves are always green. It has no worries in a year of drought and never fails to bear fruit. Jeremiah 17:7-8

DIRECTION QUESTION

Do you trust the Lord with your tears? With your children's tears? How does that make you feel?

_____

_____

_____

PRAYER PROMPT

Ask the Lord to help you look past your sufferings and look to Him. Ask Him to give you a life that resembles a tree planted beside the stream of His abundance.

_____

_____

_____

When Payton broke his hand, I was irked. He had worked so hard for baseball, and his season was over before it even started. One day when I was sharing my irritations with the Lord, I felt Him say to my heart, "You pray for your children to be overcomers. You can't be an overcomer without things to overcome."

I was convicted and asked God to give me strength for the struggle Payton was facing.

I didn't know then what was coming.

Eight months later we got a phone call that Benjamin had been in an accident. I remember hearing, "His head and neck are fine." I am still so thankful for that.

He had borrowed a friend's bike at the park and was riding fast when it looked to Benjamin that a small child was about to run in front of him. He braked hard, flipped over the handlebars, and landed on the concrete. They x-rayed his left wrist (broken), left elbow (broken) and right hand (broken). He was hurting so badly, yet as they casted him, he said, "I know I would have hurt worse if I had injured that little boy."

Isaiah 45:3 says, "And I will give you treasures hidden in the darkness—secret riches. I will do this so you may know that I am the Lord, the God of Israel, the one who calls you by name" (NLT). I believe Benjamin found his first treasure in that dark situation at that moment. In a split second, his heart had led him to choose that child rather than himself.

Suffering has the ability to draw us together unlike anything else. It was a hard time for all of us. This strong, independent teenager suddenly needed us for everything. I do not ever want him to hurt like that again, but the memory of his sister tying his shoes for him ... the memory of his brother standing up for him when someone tried to make him feel less than … well, those are memories I wouldn't trade.

We want our children to learn every lesson they can when they hurt. I am thankful for the opportunity we had to see that suffering brings a family together. It was another treasure in the darkness.

YOU-ARE-HERE QUESTION

Look back over the dark moments of this last year, can you see a treasure that came from the darkness?

_____

_____

_____

In the hard times do not forget to listen to your child. When I picked up Benjamin to take him to the ER, I wish I could tell you I was filled with compassion. I wasn't. I had questions: "Why were you on someone else's bike? Why were you not wearing a helmet? Why are we spending our night at the ER when we both had other things we wanted to be doing?"

Yes, I was asking all the questions but the truth was, I did not want his answers. Do you know what I should have been doing at that moment?

Listening.

Listen to your children. Sometimes they can help you see the treasures you are missing. There is great value in having a time each day that is screen free. I can't believe how often I am only half-way listening to the real people who are present in my life because I am communicating with people over my phone. A distracted listener is not a listener at all. The enemy would love for you to miss the big things that matter while focused on the little things that do not.

When our child appears to be in a struggle of their own making, we can react with embarrassment or anger. I learned the hard way once that those two emotions were robbing me of the chance to truly hear my child's heart. In the history of the world, no one has ever started yelling at their child and heard them respond, "Wow. There is such wisdom in what you are saying."

A distracted listener is not a listener at all.

Immediately when someone begins to yell at us, we take on a defensive posture and cease to hear words. We lose the message and receive the negative emotion. Once, one of my boys was repeatedly having a difficulty with the same person in his life, and he and I got locked in this cycle. He would share his frustration, and I would share my own frustration, saying, "Did we not just talk about this yesterday? How are you still struggling with this? Change your behavior."

My words shut him down every time. It wasn't until another person came to me and said, "I saw the way that your son is treated by so-and-so. Your child may be out of line, but he is a child. The way that adult yelled at him is unacceptable and wrong. I couldn't let you go another day without knowing the situation he is in."

I cried because my anger and embarrassment had stopped me from truly hearing my child's heart. I asked his forgiveness for not listening and for my failure to be his advocate. It's hard to push emotion aside, but sometimes we need to take a few deep breaths and ask our children, "Have I heard the whole story?"

That simple question can help your child gain perspective. It will offer them a chance to step back and recognize the part they may have played in the situation.

My mother always asked us the same question when we came to her crying and complaining about what another child did: "What were you doing right before that happened?"

It is a human tendency to tell stories that put us in a favorable light. Too many times I have rushed to judgment or to anger when I did not have the full story. Sometimes when you hear what they did first, the other person's reaction makes sense. Ask them for the full story.

We are going to make mistakes and we are going to miss important things our children try to tell us. That's why it is so sweet of God to give us the Holy Spirit who does not miss a thing. Sometimes when it gets quiet at night I will ask the Holy Spirit if I have missed anything during the day or week. Perhaps I heard a few things that I was not really listening to. So I ask Him to help me recall anything of importance that I might have overlooked. Sometimes I remember nothing, other times my mind is a rush of thoughts.

Scripture tells us that the Holy Spirit is our helper, don't forget to ask for His help.

 ## DROP-A-PIN VERSE

For our light and momentary troubles are achieving for us an eternal glory that far outweighs them all. So we fix our eyes not on what is seen, but on what is unseen, since what is seen is temporary, but what is unseen is eternal. 2 Corinthians 4:17-18

DIRECTION QUESTION

Are you intentionally listening to your children? What is your heart saying to you right now?

_____

_____

_____

PRAYER PROMPT

Ask the Lord to help you see and hear the people He has placed in your life. Ask Him to give you eyes to see that which is unseen and ears to hear that which is unspoken.

_____

_____

_____

Motherhood is a balance. How do you pull *for* someone while also pulling against? Some days feel like a battle of strong-willed child vs. strong-willed parent.

My Shelby wants to act as if everyday we start from Square One with our rules. If I draw a line in the sand and tell her not to come further, she will stand on the line. If I tell her to leave on her shoes while she is in the car seat, she will take off everything else. She awakens everyday ready for a challenge and somehow she sees me as the obstacle she needs to climb over.

I am learning what looks like a battle is actually bonding. This warrior-child and I, we're changing the world. Sometimes changing the world looks newsworthy. Sometimes it looks like a blushing, sweating mom carrying a screaming, stiff-as-a-board child across the parking lot, buckling them in and reminding them, "You and I are in this for life. We go head-to-head now so we can go heart-to-heart later. It doesn't feel like it now but I know this to be true. We end up on the same team. I'll hold on until we do."

YOU-ARE-HERE QUESTION

Where do you see yourself going head-to-head right now with the hopes that it will eventually lead to heart-to-heart?

_____

_____

_____

Struggle can be all-encompassing if we are not careful. It's so easy to lose sight of who we want to be and where we want to go.

That is why today I want to end the week by offering you some profound advice: Don't forget to have fun.

I would consider myself a fun person. I think most of my friends would confirm that to be true. Which is why it is so shocking to me that I can forget that I am supposed to be enjoying this parenting season. I get caught up in thinking I am behind in teaching my children something, and when this happens, I transform from a fun mom to a mom who is constantly lecturing, correcting, and offering advice on how my children could improve on whatever they have just done. Growing up is not easy. So having a mom who is constantly adding to everything you do can become too much real quick.

Don't be so concerned with the product that you forget the joy of the process.

Think back to when you used to imagine being a mom. I would be willing to bet that your vision for yourself as a mom was something fun or sweet, not an image of you droning on and on in a lecture. Remember to enjoy your child. Think of something that would put a smile on your child's face and do it. Work a puzzle. Learn a new sport. Make a mess. Do a craft. Not everything has to be earned; sometimes we do great and fun things with our children simply because they are our children. Spend time one-on-one with your child with the sole purpose of enjoying them. Remember, you are on the same team.

Decide right now who you want to be in the middle of difficult times and don't let yourself be derailed. Spend time today rejoicing in your role as a mother. Then rejoice in who God created in your child. Hold your baby (whether small or big) and remind them that you are for them! Have fun. Remember

Jesus is made strong in our weakness and joy can still be had in a season of pain.

Don't be so concerned with the product that you forget the joy of the process. Remember to have fun.

 ## DROP-A-PIN VERSE

In all of this you greatly rejoice, though now for a little while you may have had to suffer grief in all kinds of trials. These have come so that the proven genuineness of your faith—of greater worth than gold, which perishes even though refined by fire—may result in praise, glory and honor when Jesus Christ is revealed.

1 Peter 1:6-7

DIRECTION QUESTION

How can you engage with your child right now in a way that will bless them?

_____

_____

_____

PRAYER PROMPT

Ask the Lord to remind you of the vision He had for you as a mother when He placed these children in your home. Ask Him to give you joy, strength, and the ability to convey to your children how much they are loved.

_____

_____

_____

HOW PERFECTION WEIGHS YOU DOWN

This morning, I texted a friend, "Remember when Eden went everywhere in beautiful dresses and big bows on her head, and I felt so good about myself as a mom?"

Eden loved seeing herself dressed up, and I loved seeing myself beside her. The way she dressed made me feel like I looked put together, and I enjoyed every minute. I started teaching a class on motherhood and would tell others all the time, "You can't get your self esteem from your children. They can't carry the weight of *you.*"

Then we had Shelby Grace, our fourth child. She loves an untamed wardrobe. She loves patterns, bright colors, loud prints, and making everyone smile. She loves wearing candy cane prints in September, and is her own version of "put together." I love that too, but I also know there are some moms who look at her non-matching clothes and wonder, "Where is her mother when she gets dressed?"

I don't know why, but one morning, my imagination of the other mothers' whispers meant more to me than actually celebrating the unique way Shelby was created. I told her that she needed to change, that her clothes did not match. My words brought immediate tears to her eyes, and those tears spilled onto her cheeks.

She looked at me and said, "But I really like this outfit. Does everyone always have to match?"

Seeing her tears touched something in my heart. I love who Shelby is becoming more than I love what other people think of me. I picked her up, hugged her, and said, "I really like you. No, everyone does not have to match."

Shelby is growing up, and so am I.

YOU-ARE-HERE QUESTION

Is there an area where you may be basing your self esteem on something other than who you are in Christ?

_____

_____

_____

Each of us comes into motherhood hoping to get it right. We read the articles. We "Google" anything that we don't know. We want to be good mothers. Yet, when it comes to what feels like the most important job in our life, we don't always know what we're doing. It takes courage to admit that. Sometimes our children want to take a different route than the one we would choose.

The children in your home are there because the Lord intended to equip you to parent them. Whether they were knit together in your womb, adopted, fostered, or brought to you in any other way ... the Lord knew that they would end up in your care. He is ready to help you raise up your child to His glory.

> *Everything of value will have*
> *an obstacle placed in front of it.*

Our all-knowing, all-seeing God created this earth. All that we have been able to explore in space and beyond, was created by Him. He could have, in His power, made each of us perfect. He could have put a child in our home that we would never disagree with. He could have set us up to parent without challenge. Have you thought about that? Perfection was a possibility in His hands ...

Yet He allowed us to have flaws. He formed both us and our children in a way that would cause all of us to grow. He allowed us to have qualities in ourselves that He knew we would not like. We are imperfect, but our world has set forth Perfection as the goal. As a result, we alter, edit, fake, and filter. Everything of value will have an obstacle placed in front of it. Could it be that the true value in life is acknowledging our imperfection?

Let's remove the obstacles.

We want to acknowledge our flaws and our Jesus who helps us overcome them. The mistakes we make are redeemable. Your life, your marriage, your parenting, your friendships, everything about you was intended to point others to the power of God and the hope that He brings. How can we be known as overcomers in Christ if we position ourselves as people who have nothing to overcome? Satan wants us to live our lives focused on ourselves, our mistakes, and things we wish were different. Jesus wants you to see the value in who you are right now. He wants you to see the beauty in life and the various personalities represented in your family.

Our self esteem isn't based on the way our kids dress, or the way they behave, or whether they eat their vegetables, or if they sleep through the night. Our worth is not determined by our performance; it is based on the unchanging love of Christ. He led a perfect life so that we would never have to feel the pressure of perfection.

 DROP-A-PIN VERSE

And by His one perfect sacrifice He made us perfectly holy and complete for all time. Hebrews 10:14 TPT

DIRECTION QUESTION

Is there an area where you have been looking for perfection that you are ready to surrender to Him?

_____

_____

_____

PRAYER PROMPT

Ask the Lord to give you eyes to see your strength and give you a heart that rejoices in His creation in you and in your children.

_____

_____

_____

When Payton was starting middle school, I told him how important it was that he always wear pants or shorts with a belt.

"Why?" he would ask.

My response was always the same, "There are mean kids in middle school, and sometimes they will try to pull your pants down when you least expect it."

I think if there were an award for the most discouraging speech you could give your child before the start of middle school, I would win it. All of you with children who have not yet reached middle school just shuddered at the thought.

Several weeks later, Payton came home and said, "I am wearing athletic shorts to school tomorrow, and I will probably never wear a belt again. I have been in middle school for weeks now, and I have not seen one person get their pants pulled down. Where did you hear your stories?"

It was at this point that I admitted I had not heard that story about his particular middle school at all. I had lived it out in *mine*. And 30 years later, I was trying to help my son write a better story for his middle school experience than I'd had. I was overparenting, big time. Because I'd had a bad experience, I wanted to do everything possible to protect my child from having the same one. In fact, I wanted him to have the *perfect* middle school experience. Now I realize that was a silly goal. A perfect middle school experience doesn't exist for anyone. My own fear and insecurity can't be the foundation upon which I build advice for my child. Only Jesus is secure.

YOU-ARE-HERE QUESTION

Have you ever intentionally or unintentionally passed on a fear to one of your children?

_____

_____

_____

Satan wants us to live our lives focused on ourselves. He knows well the traps of overparenting. These traps usually come when we are thinking about life from one of three perspectives:

1. I want my child to have what I didn't have.
2. I want my child to have exactly what I had.
3. I want my child to avoid any and all pain.

The enemy knows if he can paralyze us with any one of those pursuits he gains temporary victory over us. Perfection is Satan's attempt to cage what the Lord has set free. When you live your life focused on an unattainable goal, it is time wasted.

> *Perfection is Satan's attempt to cage what the Lord has set free.*

Here are some ways to check yourself:

- What is your focus right now?
- Are you taking time to praise God?
- What are you thanking God for right now? Name the top five things. (Gratitude so often brings life back into focus.)

Anytime you are feeling burdened by the weight of motherhood, ask yourself, "Is it a burden from God or the enemy?" A burden from God comes with an empowering hope that He can use you to make a difference. A burden from Satan sucks at your strength and causes you to doubt yourself and your heavenly father.

Grace is the heart language of Christ. He is the God who reaches out for His people. When we truly realize that He can be trusted, it changes the way that we look, and God is glorified.

DROP-A-PIN VERSE

So you have not received a spirit that makes you fearful slaves. Instead, you received God's Spirit when he adopted you as his own children. Now we call him, "Abba, Father."   Romans 8:15 NLT

DIRECTION QUESTION

Where are you needing to be released from bondage?

_____

_____

_____

PRAYER PROMPT

Ask the Lord to break any bonds of fear that have been passed down to you. Ask the Lord to show you where the pursuit of perfection in your child or in their story might be causing you to act irrationally.

_____

_____

_____

Have you ever worked so hard to make something special for your child, only to find yourself bubbling over with anger rather than joy? Am I the only one who has said in a raised voice, "I WAS TRYING TO DO SOMETHING SPECIAL FOR YOU!"

My daughter Eden had been faithful with her chore chart and had earned $20 over the summer. That felt like a fortune to her 4-year-old self. I told her we would stop and get a cake pop and milk at a coffee shop on our way to the store to spend her money. She was so sweet and appreciative while we were getting the treats that even the barista said, "What a precious child."

I wholeheartedly agreed. Those kinds of moments fill up a mom's heart.

We happily walked into the store and started looking at toys. Everything was going well until Eden fell in love with a toy that was $80. Tony and I had already agreed we would be willing to give some extra to cover tax, etc ... but an extra $60 was not in the plan or our budget. I told my precious, appreciative child that she would need to find another toy.

She looked at me, repeating that she had already found the toy she wanted.

I smiled at her, explained basic math, and said, "If you want to spend your twenty dollars, you are going to need to look for a different toy."

Other people on the aisle were starting to notice my conversation with Eden. I looked up at them, and they all smiled. I smiled back.

That is when that angelic little face looked right at me and said, "I want *this one*. If you won't get it for me, I will squirt this milk on you." She pointed her boxed milk at me like a weapon.

I lowered my voice and said. "If you do that, Eden, I can assure you that you will regret it." Oblivious to threats, she hosed me with her milk.

The people on the aisle gasped.

I was livid. My mind raced with anger, embarrassment, and a strong desire to get out of there as fast as I could. Something in me wanted to save my pride and let the people who had witnessed this moment know that I actually am a decent parent. I wanted to ask the spectators to go talk to the barista at the front of the store for confirmation that this child was not a tiny diva. I wanted to yell at her for humiliating me. But the Holy Spirit gripped my heart at the exact moment I gripped Eden's arm. He said, "Choose Eden over that group of strangers. Parent *her*, not the moment."

So I whispered, "We are leaving without a toy. Right now."

My hair was still dripping with milk as I carried her screaming, from the back of the store to the front doors. Thank you God for a Spirit that speaks louder than a screaming child and reminds us to choose love over pride.

YOU-ARE-HERE QUESTION

Have you ever found yourself parenting out of embarrassment rather than love for your child? What did that look like?

_____

_____

_____

Here are some ways we are trying to look more like Jesus around our house (and in the store):

- **We are not looking for perfection in our children.** The Lord had one perfect Son. The rest of us are called to be reflections of perfection, not the real thing. Our goal is to look more like the Savior, not be Him. There is freedom in that truth for both ourselves and our children. We are going to mess up. The Lord knew that. He gave Jesus so that we could get back up and keep going. We honor Him in that response.

> Our goal is to look more like
> the Savior, not **be** Him.

- **We want to be known for extending grace and mercy.** We have high expectations for our children. But one of those expectations is that our children are going to mess up. A lot. We are looking to find the balance of high expectations and grace. Lord, help us.
- **We communicate expectations and consequences clearly.** We may be caught off guard by our children's choice of behavior, but our children are not caught off guard by our response. I am a work in progress, but I try to be consistent. I don't want my children to live in fear of what kind of mom might show up when they've made a mistake.

God's glory is revealed through flaws and through overcoming them. He brings beauty from ashes, from spilled milk, from brokenness, from annoying personality traits, and from embarrassments in stores. He's great at taking what we have and using it to bless those around us.

In Matthew 14, Jesus is preaching out in the country to a large crowd. Night is falling and His disciples are getting worried. They are feeling pressure. They know these people need to eat so the disciples encourage Jesus, "Dismiss the people so they can go to the villages and get some supper."

But Jesus was not feeling the same pressure, He knew every person in the audience; He had been a part of creating them. He knew when they were formed that someday they would have to eat. He was not surprised by their need.

So our Jesus, unfazed, responds, "There is no need to dismiss them. You feed them supper."

The disciples reply, " All we have are five loaves of bread and two fish." It is only enough for one person's lunch. What would they do for the 4,999 others?

Oh, that each of us would hear Jesus' response deep in our souls. He says, "Bring me what you have."

Still confused, they do.

Then He blesses it, and over five thousand are fed.

That's our God. He takes what we have, blesses it, and turns a lunch box into a feast. Are you struggling today? Feeling pressure? Feeling overwhelmed?

The same Jesus who worked that miracle is ready to work another one.

Bring Him what you have.

 ## DROP-A-PIN VERSE

> *Bring all who claim me as their God, for I have made them for my glory. It was I who created them.* Isaiah 43:7 NLT

DIRECTION QUESTION

In what area is Jesus asking you to bring Him what you have?

_____

_____

_____

PRAYER PROMPT

Ask the Lord to help your life reflect His glory and to let your heart rest in the work that He is doing in you.

_____

_____

_____

A few months ago one of our rabbits, Sophia, had babies. Our excitement quickly led to panic when she killed them.

In the midst of our mortification, I realized someone had to clean up the crime scene. It was another "mom assignment" you don't expect. I got busy, and as I was gagging, I looked over to ask Eden what she was doing. She was kneeling with her hands and head on Sophia.

Overcome with emotion, she said, "I'm asking God to remind Sophia that there is good in her, that she was created to love. She's forgotten why she's here."

I think I rolled my eyes. I easily forget to see past a situation and look for the good. Sometimes we only see what's gone wrong. But the Lord sees imperfections and remembers He made a plan to cover them.

The other day when I picked up Eden at art camp she showed me she had made a sculpture of—you guessed it—Sophia the Killer Rabbit.

On the way home I asked, "Why Sophia? You have other pets that only have a history of kindness."

"Mom," she answered, "Sophia *is* kind, she just forgets who she is in stressful situations. I choose to remember what's good and love her."

This time, her words caught my heart. I am so thankful for a God who looks past my imperfection, chooses to see what is good, and loves me.

And when you come to our house and notice a certain rabbit sculpture in a prominent place, you will know I'm reminding myself to focus on the good.

YOU-ARE-HERE QUESTION

Have you had any moments when you have forgotten who you are as a mom?

_____

_____

_____

I often think of Moses' mothers. Both of them saw something special in Moses at an early age. Exodus 2:2 tells us Moses' birth mom recognized immediately that he was "a fine child" and determined to protect him from the death sentence that Pharaoh had imposed on the Hebrew babies.

Moses' adoptive mom, Pharaoh's daughter, recognized something in the baby floating in the river that made her think it was worth defying her father's orders as well. Both women believed this child was going to do something great. It strikes me that most likely both of Moses' mothers went to their graves thinking that they had been wrong.

By age 40, Moses did not look like he was going to be great. He had killed an Egyptian and fled the country. It is likely neither mother ever saw him again. Moses doesn't enter into the climax of his career until he is 80. At that time, God brings a broken and flawed man out of the desert to lead the Lord's people. Moses' mothers may have missed seeing it, but God's plan was not thwarted by Moses' mistakes.

As a mother, you have to remember that the Lord has a plan that cannot be stopped by our sin or our children's sin. Like Sophia the Killer Rabbit, we were created to love. Our children will make mistakes. We can model for them how mistakes can be something that presses us closer to the Lord rather than something that pushes us away. Satan wants to come to us in our sin and tell us, "Stay away from God, He is so disappointed in you."

> *Our sins are not without consequence,*
> *but our God is not without love.*

Yet God longs to be like brokenhearted Eden that day in the backyard, pulling Sophia close and whispering "Remember who you are."

Our sins are not without consequence, but our God is not without love.

As parents we can show our children love as well. After a consequence is given, allow some time and then—always—immerse your children in love. Just as your Heavenly Father calls you back through Christ, call your children back into your arms. You don't serve a God who gives you the silent treatment.

 ## DROP-A-PIN VERSE

I know that you can do anything, and no one can stop you.

Job 42:2 NLT

DIRECTION QUESTION

Is there a sin in your past or in the past of someone you love that you keep focusing on?

_____

_____

_____

PRAYER PROMPT

Confess to the Lord your desire to focus on His ability rather than your flaws. Ask Him to bring to your mind someone else who needs this reminder. Pray for them that this truth would take deep root in their heart.

_____

_____

_____

One morning I woke up early and realized that I had not gotten the needed supplies for my kids to make their sandwiches for the day. I looked at the clock, and seeing I was still in the 4 a.m. hour, I knew I had plenty of time to run to the grocery store before the kids woke up. Making sure I had my wallet, I headed out the door. I was a mom-on-a-mission, and I was focused.

There was only one problem. I thought our local grocery store was a 24-hour store. So when the sliding doors would not open, I assumed they were broken. That is why I worked my fingers into the crack and pried them open.

Sure, I noticed the lights were dim, but I thought it was due to energy-saving lighting used when there were not a lot of customers. I grabbed my grocery basket and walked directly to the lunch meat. I thought I was getting stuff for sandwiches, but, as it turns out, I was breaking and entering. The security guard came up to me and asked if I knew I was trespassing in a closed store.

It took me a few minutes to even wrap my mind around what he was saying. I was disoriented because I had made so many assumptions, all of which lined up with my mission, that even when the night manager was nicely explaining why I should not be there, I was nicely explaining why I should.

Eventually, I got it. The manager was gracious to me, and the police were not called. She understood I was a mom-on-a-mission. We both had a good laugh, and I stopped blushing about six hours later.

YOU-ARE-HERE QUESTION

Have you ever felt so right that it was completely disorienting to find out you were wrong?

_____

_____

_____

One of my favorite things about Jesus is looking at the men He chose to be close to while He was here on earth. He chose imperfect men. He chose men who had tempers, men who were arrogant, men who wrestled with doubt, and men who got scared easily. If I had been the one choosing I would've chosen men who were well spoken, who carried themselves in a way that people respected. I would have chosen completely different people than Jesus did.

And I would have been wrong.

Jesus knew what his life on earth was to be about, and He chose people just like you and me to help Him accomplish His mission. He knew better than anyone what it would take to introduce people to His Father in a way that would not just change their eternity, but change their daily lives, as well. He had intimate knowledge of the apostles' imperfections and chose them anyway. Broken and flawed people are His favorite. Isn't that wildly comforting? We serve a God who seeks us out.

Broken and flawed people are His favorite.

There are going to be moments when you doubt the Lord's choice of you as your child's mother. You may be confident that your friend down the street could be a better mom than you. When that night manager was explaining to me why I shouldn't be in the grocery store I stood there and slowly realized the narrative in my head was wrong. I was somewhere I was not supposed to be. I pray when you doubt yourself as a mom you will realize the same thing. The narrative that has you questioning yourself is somewhere you are not supposed to be.

Hebrews 13:8 says, "Jesus Christ is the same yesterday and today and forever." Long ago, Jesus chose to hang out with those with weakness, and today He is still making the same choice. When you wonder if there might be someone better equipped to be the mother of your children, Jesus responds, "No! It's *you*, exactly as you are, looking to Me and allowing Me to work through you!"

When we take hold of Jesus we push aside the illusion of perfection and say, "I want to be exactly who I am. My imperfections don't separate me from God, they actually draw Him near."

DROP-A-PIN VERSE

I am not saying that I have this all together, that I have it made. But I am well on my way, reaching out for Christ, who has so wondrously reached out for me. Friends, don't get me wrong: By no means do I count myself an expert in all of this, but I've got my eye on the goal, where God is beckoning us onward—to Jesus. I'm off and running and I'm not turning back.

Philippians 3:12-14 MSG

DIRECTION QUESTION

Is there a story that you keep writing in your head that is based on the lies of the enemy?

_____

_____

_____

PRAYER PROMPT

Ask the Lord to show you a scripture that you can hang onto when you begin to doubt. Ask Him for His help in believing His truth over the lies of the enemy.

_____

_____

_____

How to Make Family Goals

DAY 1

When our family was setting our yearly goals once, Eden said, "I want the jealous part of my heart to go away. I hope the part of me that sees other people getting good things and wishes that was me instead will leave. I want to learn to cheer for others without always thinking about myself first."

She has a way of saying things that make the rest of us put down our pencils and say, "That sounds good for me too."

She makes our whole family better by just being her. She is so self aware that she knows where her heart is and where she wants it to go. Eden is tender, and I love that she is already thinking of ways the Lord can change her.

I wish I had been that way as a child.

Because I wasn't self-aware and seeking improvement way back then, I ended up as an adult who still loses things. Sigh. I laugh and blame it on the fact that my mind is in constant motion, and often I am going through my life on autopilot, without any thought on what I am actually doing. Thanks be to God, I married a man who is a continual display of God's mercy.

One memorable night, we were supposed to be attending a Texas Ranger's baseball game. After two hours of frantic searching, it became apparent I was not going to be able to locate our tickets. I looked at Tony and said, "I know there are a million things you would like to say to me and every single one of them is justified."

Tony just smiled and asked where I wanted to go for dinner.

Here's the truth. When we first got married, Tony did not react that way, but the Lord is at work in his life. In that moment, when he chose not to comment on my carelessness, I saw the power of God in him.

I want that same power to be at work in me. Thankfully, I see the Lord changing me and my ability to focus on the little things. I have had the same pair of sunglasses for a while, and that is no small victory. Every night I pay attention to where I put them. I may never be as organized as Tony, but the Lord is moving in and through me, and it's all to His glory. I had to take a hard look at where I was and make the decision I did not want to stay there any longer. I wasn't satisfied with saying, "That's just who I am."

I had to set some goals so I could get out of the pattern of misplacing things.

YOU-ARE-HERE QUESTION

Is there a part of you that for too long you have excused as "that's just who I am," when it could be an opportunity for you to display God's glory?

_____

_____

_____

Part of goal-setting is acknowledging where you are. It's why people get on a scale and know their weight before they start eating right. It's why people look at their grades before they set the goal of being top of the class. You have to see where you are before you can know where you are going. You also have to know why you want something in order to stay motivated to get it.

Goals give us purpose and remind us of who we want to be. In our relationship with God, we should be ever changing, growing closer each day to being who He created. We want to know Christ, not just as our Savior but as our life-giving, life-changing friend.

Sometimes, when people talk about goals it can be more discouraging than encouraging. It is easier to focus on what you don't have than what you do. That is because the enemy is always at work. He wants you to be aimless in your life. He wants to discourage you with the thought that where you are is where you will always be. Make sure you are listening to the tone of the voice in your head. The Lord brings conviction and the hope of change. Satan brings guilt and a feeling of despair that things have already gone too far. Don't listen to him.

Families that set goals together experience three things:

1. They know where they are going.
2. They recognize obstacles in their path.
3. They come together as a team.

In a culture where life moves fast, a family can constantly be living in survival mode. Survival mode may look like, "Let's get everyone up, dressed, fed, where they need to be, then back home, fed, and to bed so we have the energy to do it all over again tomorrow." There will be seasons in every parent's life when they are forced to move into survival mode. If we are not aware and careful though, survival mode can rob us of years of our life. We know this deep in our hearts.

As parents, we have to clarify, "Where do we want our family to end up?"

If you are married, it's important that you and your spouse come to agreement in this area. I also want to acknowledge the mothers who do not have a supportive or like-minded spouse. I believe the Lord will grant you supernatural wisdom, strength, and ability for the task before you.

Now for the Brooks, as a Bible-believing family, our ultimate goal is that we would all end up together with Jesus in the Presence of God. If that is the ultimate goal, it will surface in our daily decisions. Is the majority of how we spend our time drawing us to that end?

Often when a family goes to make a budget or spending plan, they record their current spending for a month. When you have a month or more of receipts, you start seeing your priorities as a family. If convenience is a priority, there will be money spent on fast food. If activity is a priority, the receipts will reflect that. We all know that spending habits reflect values. The receipts do not lie.

Just as you track where your family spends money, it will be helpful for you to start looking at how your family spends time. Where is your time going each month?

Regarding things like character traits, money, and time, what are the qualities you see in your family now? What are the qualities you want to see in your family in the future?

> *A family goal often starts by being*
> *a personal goal for the parent.*

Tony and I have decided that we want our children to value being a team. As we reflect on where we are and project where we want to be, we want the majority of our goals to bring us together as a team.

Family goals are a place for you to examine yourself as an individual. I have had to acknowledge that it is going to be hard for me to say, "I want my children to eat healthy," if I am not willing to eat healthy myself. I can't say, "We are a family that doesn't yell in arguments," if I am consistently doing the opposite.

We cannot expect what we do not model. A family goal often starts by being a personal goal for the parent.

Goals should be something that bonds hearts as we all work towards reaching it together.

DROP-A-PIN VERSE

Brothers and sisters, I do not consider myself yet to have taken hold of it. But one thing I do: Forgetting what is behind and straining towards what is ahead, I press on toward the goal to win the prize for which God has called me heavenward in Christ Jesus.

Philippians 3:13-14

DIRECTION QUESTION

What are the top three goals you have for your family? Do you and your spouse both agree on the top three?

_____

_____

_____

PRAYER PROMPT

Ask the Lord to give you a vision for where your family is and where it could be. Ask Him to bring you and your family members into agreement.

_____

_____

_____

Shelby feels everything with her whole heart. When she was a toddler, any strong emotions brought tears. If I woke her up before she was ready, she would cry. If we were having pancakes, and she did not want them, she would cry. If the cupcake she was given at preschool was chocolate rather than vanilla ... once again, tears. There was nothing wrong with Shelby's emotions—I too love a vanilla cupcake—but we had to set some goals for how she was going to express herself.

That's why we started Shelby's "You can only cry two times a day" Rule.

Granted, if actual pain was involved, that did not count. But for anything other than a scraped knee or similar injury, it was time to train how she handled those emotions.

And so it went ...

When I would wake her up and see her wrinkle that brow, I would whisper, "You don't want to use a cry this early do you?"

She would shake her head and continue on with the morning.

When she would come to breakfast, see pancakes and pause before the whimper, I would whisper, "Sister, don't waste a cry over these."

She would agree and eat the pancakes. Eventually, she even realized she *likes* pancakes.

Seeing her transformation showed us that it wasn't that everything made Shelby sad, it was that Shelby used tears to express everything. It seems silly now, but part of Shelby's great personality is her ability to feel deeply. However, we were missing out on the joy of that because her constant crying became a problem. We had to set some goals to help Shelby manage her tears, and in the process, we also helped Shelby learn about herself.

I have had to learn about myself as well. My boys love sports. One of my favorite things is watching them play. I pride myself on cheering for them so I was shocked when Payton pulled me aside after a game. He said, "Mom, why do you yell things that call attention to something I am already attempting? Why yell, 'Make your free throw?' You know that's what I am trying to do. It's embarrassing. Besides, if I miss, it makes me think I let down my team *and* my mom. I'd rather you just cheered for me and let me know you are there whether I make a shot or not."

> *If you are trying to bless,*
> *make sure it doesn't add stress.*

Just like Shelby had to set the goal to manage her tears, I needed to set the goal to manage my words. If you are trying to bless, make sure it doesn't add stress. I still yell for my children, and sometimes I still get it wrong. But these days I focus on my goal. I want my children to know I am there, and I support them.

Their coach knows the game so I let him shout the instructions. I know their hearts so I just love them loud.

YOU-ARE-HERE QUESTION

Have you ever tried to bless someone, and they did not receive it as a blessing?

_____

_____

_____

As you are working to set goals, remember to set some long-term goals along with the short-term ones. Children (and their parents!) feel encouraged by seeing forward movement.

When we set the goal for Shelby to only have two cries a day, we said that everyday she made it, she got a sticker on the calendar. When she accumulated five days worth of stickers, we celebrated by playing a game together or getting her a small prize. That was helpful in redirecting her. Often, I could see where she was about to go before she even knew. So I would remind her about her goal.

In the same way, when I head to a sporting event to watch Payton, I remind myself of my goal. At first, I would ask Tony and my friends to hold me accountable. One time, I actually brought an apple that I could eat to keep my mouth occupied. I didn't want to start yelling my "State the Obvious" faux encouragement again.

Do not underestimate small goals like these. Short-term goals are developing life-long skills. When Shelby is able to express herself in ways that do not involve tears, it blesses others. And when Payton is an adult, I know he will not be encouraged by me yelling, "Get a job!"

I am training myself now to bless him later. Years from now, I want him to know:

I am still here, and I am still for you.

We often set short term goals that we hope will turn into long-term habits. Some easy steps are:

1. **Select a timeframe.** Start small. Choose a way for your child to mark progress over time (X on the calendar, paper chain, sticker etc...)

2. **Avoid comparison.** Ask the Lord to help you in the process of setting goals. You may want to get ideas from other families, but your family's goals should be uniquely yours. The Lord is going to do a one-of-a-kind work in your family so don't frustrate the process by involving comparison.

3. **Offer grace, grace, and more grace.** Not reaching a goal in a certain time frame does not mean it will not be met, it means we need more time, more Jesus, more love. Goal-setting should NOT be something that divides a family or a relationship; it should be something that unites.

4. **Be creative.** Is your goal family unity? Start walking together. Start playing board games. Start reading together, cooking together, doing laundry together. Ask the Lord to help you be creative. Ask the Lord to reveal to you, your spouse and your children ways in which you can reach your goal. When your children make a suggestion, listen to them. Try it.

5. **Keep things simple.** Baby steps are important. You did not make your infant feel bad about crawling. Don't allow yourself to feel bad if it appears your family is crawling towards a goal. We all start that way. You crawl before you walk.

6. **Encourage yourself and encourage each other.** As you and your family work towards reaching goals, make sure you shower the process with encouragement.

7. **Remember what it's all about.** No one wants to reach a goal and have her family more divided than ever. Pray for unity and then model it. Remember, you are not in a race

with any other family. We are all striving to look more like Christ, and He has a different timeline and process for each of us.

DROP-A-PIN VERSE

Trust in the Lord with all your heart and lean not on your own understanding; in all your ways acknowledge Him and He will make your paths straight. Proverbs 3:5-6

DIRECTION QUESTION

Have you thought about asking your children if there is a particular way you could bring encouragement to them? These types of honest conversations lay a foundation for a lifetime of knowing how to bless your people.

_____

_____

_____

PRAYER PROMPT

The Lord knows exactly what your people need. Ask Him to lead you in this process and grow you in your ability to love each other.

_____

_____

_____

One day I was complaining to Tony about how much I dislike taking down Christmas decor in our home.

He shrugged and said, "Make the boys do it."

It was that easy. For the past few years the Brooks brothers have packed and stored away all our Christmas decor. Is anything broken in the process? If it is, I don't find out until 11 months later. I call that a success. Over the years a few things have broken, but even if I had taken down the Christmas decor myself, a few things would have been broken. As you support your children, remember to extend the same grace to them that you would want extended to yourself in the same situation. Don't forget that part of building confidence is allowing your children to take on big tasks and accomplish them. I choose not to worry about the possibility of broken decor, and instead be thankful that my sons are contributing to our family in this simple way.

That is not to say that they always *want* to contribute.

Tony's ongoing theme for them is, "You can, and you will." Tony and I feel enthusiasm for that theme, and it is always off the charts. The boys' enthusiasm has yet to register.

Letting them grow into being hard workers reminds me of the day I set off on a bike ride with Shelby. She was riding, and I was jogging beside her. She had been doing so well, and we were ambitious with the wind at our back.

Oh, how things changed.

I wish I had a picture or a video of myself carrying Shelby and her bike for at least the last mile back to our home. It was not the ending I had imagined when we started our journey, that is for sure. While I mentally berated myself for thinking we could go so far from home, Shelby whispered in my ear, "Brooks girls don't give up. You can do this."

I would have rolled my eyes if I could have mustered the energy. Her legs may have gotten tired but her heart never stopped encouraging.

Carrying Shelby worked because she was four and still learning to follow through. But as mothers our expectations should grow as our children do. My teenage sons are able to take on more responsibility each year, and I am going to expect them to do so. Indeed, that is part of growing up. I no longer need to carry my sons in areas where they should be following through with work.

YOU-ARE-HERE QUESTION

How are you at delegating jobs in your home to others? What's a small or large job that you are ready to pass on to the next generation?

_____

_____

_____

Part of setting goals is letting go and letting your children try things on their own. I have to remind myself of this: Part of our purpose as parents is to work ourselves out of a job. I have to place a higher value on allowing my children to learn than on getting the job done perfectly.

> *Part of our purpose as parents is to work ourselves out of a job.*

As we proceed in orienting our life with family goals, we remember to start with prayer. The Lord has a direction He would like for you to go as a family. Ask Him to show it to you, including the age at which your children should start setting goals of their own. You will have some goals that are for your entire family and some that are for each member as individuals. Ask the Lord to show you where your focus should be in each area and with each person.

Remind yourself that goals for your children will look different because each of them are different. Some goals are very specific and measurable, others look more like a general direction you want your life to go.

For instance, one of our boys has written down "Self Control" as a goal. That is not specific or measurable; it is a general direction. We talk about this daily. He desires self-control in his life, but it does not come naturally. He has to remind himself each morning that his long-term goal at school is to learn, so he has to set the short-term goal of self-control in each moment. This child wants to enjoy school and have fun with his friends, but he also, after being "inspired by his parents," wants to leave school with grades that reflect what he is learning.

One of our boys tends to value perfection in his work. He has written down "Relax" as a goal. This child has to remind himself that while grades are important, he also wants to form good relationships. He is determined to remind himself throughout the day to laugh and enjoy himself.

Do you see how those goals are unique to the individual? Each child has a unique gift from the Lord in their personality. We can help them set goals that use those gifts to the fullest; we can also help them set goals that cause them to reach outside of who they are naturally. Encourage your children to reach beyond themselves. You want them to learn early to lean into Jesus.

I am not a good listener by nature, but to be a good friend, which is a goal of mine, I have had to learn this trait. I can assure you that is to the Lord's glory; He knows my desire to talk. The same power He used to shut the mouths of the lions in the den is at work in my life. As a result, I am listening more.

Good goals are going to cause you and your family to stretch.

 ## DROP-A-PIN VERSE

Commit to the Lord whatever you do, and He will establish your plans. Proverbs 16:3

DIRECTION QUESTION

Where is your heart? Where do you want it to be? Is there a direction goal you would like to set for the members of your family?

_____

_____

_____

PRAYER PROMPT

Ask the Lord to help you learn the gift of stretching and growing in your flexibility.

_____

_____

_____

Last week Shelby had a ferocious stomach bug. At one point when I was walking by with my arms full of laundry, she said, "My body feels like it's healing when it holds your hand."

So we sat holding hands for the better part of two days. She was watching TV, I was watching her.

At the end of day two, she was feeling better and said, "What do I do when I grow up, and I can't hold your hand?"

I told her, "I'll always hold your hand, but if for some reason I can't … you know how to hold onto Jesus."

She smiled, said, "I sure do," and went back to watching *Barbie: Life in the Dream House*. Meanwhile, I choked back my tears.

In *The Message*, Psalm 91:14 reads, "'If you'll hold on to me for dear life,' says God, 'I'll get you out of any trouble. I'll give you the best of care if you'll only get to know and trust me. Call me and I'll answer, be at your side in bad times.'"

There are so many things I want for my children, but learning to call out to the Lord is at the top of my list. May they always know their Heavenly Father hears their voice and responds to their cries.

May they always know they can hold His hand.

YOU-ARE-HERE QUESTION

In what ways do you hold onto God? How can you strengthen your grip on His promises?

_____

_____

_____

Sometimes we make things too hard. Don't fall into that trap as you begin to get a vision of where you would like for your family to go.

- Set attainable goals.
- Keep goals simple, yet challenging.
- Be prepared for some tension in the pursuit of a goal.
- Stay focused on your goal.
- Ask for help or reinforcement to reach a goal.

We all like the "After" photos in workout programs, but the hard work and discipline that went into making those "After" pictures is not visible in the picture itself. Your "Before" and your "After" are going to involve a lot of hard work in the middle.

> *Your "Before" and your "After" are going to involve a lot of hard work in the middle.*

 DROP-A-PIN VERSE

Brothers and sisters, I do not consider myself yet to have taken hold of it. But one thing I do: Forgetting what is behind and straining towards what is ahead, I press on toward the goal to win the prize for which God has called me heavenward in Christ Jesus.

Philippians 3:13-14

DIRECTION QUESTION

Is there a goal for you or your family that feels so hard, you don't even want to write it down?

_____

_____

_____

PRAYER PROMPT

Ask the Lord to help you align your goals with His.

_____

_____

_____

DAY 5

While I was checking Shelby's first grade school work, I noticed that one of the words that she was asked to use in a sentence was "sin." She used it in an unusual way.

I asked her, "What do you mean you *sin* to your mom? You sin against God but you don't sin to me."

"No, I totally do. Like, when you tell me to get my room cleaned up and then walk out. I used to say, 'She is so dumb.' Then one time I heard God say, 'Shelby, that is not true, and that is a sin.' I'm doing better, but I used to sin to you all the time."

As a mom, you grab encouragement wherever you can get it. My take away from that conversation?

Shelby is listening to the Lord.

One of my goals is to grow in being unoffendable. When I was a younger mom, much of my self esteem was wrapped up in how my children acted and responded to me. Shelby's explanation that day made me laugh. In the past, the same words would have made me sad and caused me to question myself. No more. I want my child to grow, unfettered by my feelings. I want her to be able to share how the Lord is changing her in every way, even in relation to her feelings about me. I am learning to look for the good in all things because the enemy works so hard to make sure I notice the negative. So yes, I noticed my daughter called me *dumb*, but I also noticed my Heavenly Father defended me, and my daughter heard His voice.

Grace and mercy. He is growing us all.

Are you noticing the small improvements in others? Are you noticing the small improvements in yourself?

_____

_____

_____

One of the things that I love and admire about my husband is his daily preparation. Each day as he prepares to leave for work, he has a bag sitting right beside his phone and keys. Without looking, I can tell you what is inside of that bag: A protein shake, a bag of mixed nuts, and a paleo bar. Why does he have these things? Because he anticipates his hunger, and he wants to be ready for it. As you set goals for your family, I want you to anticipate your hunger and be ready for it. Remember to pack some power for the journey. Here are a few verses you might want to take along with you:

- **Nehemiah 8:10** reminds us that "the joy of the Lord is your strength." Hold onto that promise. What Nehemiah is telling us is that we are God's joy. Just as you look at your sleeping child and wonder how you could be so blessed to have them as your very own, so our Heavenly Father feels this about us. Even when you stumble and miss your goals, you remain the joy of your Heavenly Father's heart. Let that bring you strength.
- **Lamentations 3:22-24** says, "Because of the Lord's great love we are not consumed, for his compassions never fail. They are new every morning; great is your faithfulness. I say to myself, 'The Lord is my portion; therefore I will wait for him.'" I love this verse. I am slowly becoming more

patient as I learn to wait on the Lord. He is enough for me. When I am feeling overwhelmed by life, I whisper aloud, "I will not be consumed." My heart is strengthened when I hear it.

- **John 10:10** says, "The thief comes only to steal, kill and destroy; I have come that they may have life and have it to the full." These are Jesus' words to you. He offers you a warning about our enemy so that you can be aware of his schemes and then he offers you comfort. He has come that you might still experience the fullness of life he has for you. He knew that as a mother there would be some hard times, but he also knew that you would have the opportunity in him to experience the incredible gift of a joy filled, aching with love heart. Jesus intended for this life to be full. Hold onto that hope.

- **Psalm 127:1** says, "Unless the Lord builds the house, the builders labor in vain." This verse reminds me of why I want to partner with the Lord in the goal-setting, goal-reaching process. I want a home and family that is centered on God. We want Jesus as our firm foundation because he is the only thing that will hold.

Anticipate that you and your family will need to lean into the Lord in order to meet your goals.

Ask for His help. Hold to His hand. Listen for His voice. He is with you.

Anticipate that you and your family will need to lean into the Lord in order to meet your goals.

DROP-A-PIN VERSE

So do not throw away your confidence; it will be richly rewarded.
You need to persevere so that when you have done the will of God,
you will receive what He has promised. Hebrews 10:35-36

DIRECTION QUESTION

What does your perseverance look like? Are you strong in that
trait or do you need to develop in it?

_____

_____

_____

PRAYER PROMPT

Ask the Lord to help you be patient as we wait for Him to bring
change to your family.

_____

_____

_____

Why Boldness
Matters

DAY 1

We thought we were completely prepared for our first baby. Clothes were washed, diapers were organized, and we had aced the birthing class. Our baby's nursery was exactly how we wanted it.

Because I was confident that there was nothing more we could have done to get ready for this child, I was stunned to find myself a bawling mess the first night we came home from the hospital.

I was exhausted and felt desperate for sleep, but for the first time in my life, I had someone who was dependent on me for nourishment. This made me cry even more. My husband and my mother were doing everything they could to help in this process but the facts were: My baby needed me. At one point, I was crying to my mom in the wee hours of the morning, telling her that I wasn't sure if I was cut out to be a mom.

"I am tired. My body is sore. I need sleep. I do not know how I'll make it if I have to get up every three hours to feed my son."

My mom, who is quite skilled at speaking the truth in love, said boldly, "You are acting like this is an option. You *can* do this, and you *will*. Now let's do it."

I needed that push. A reminder that I was able. A reminder that generations of mothers that had gone ahead of me, and they also were tired, frazzled, and unsure. The feeling of "I have never wanted to do something more right than raise this child" is strong. When we are hit with waves of uncertainty, exhaustion, and emotion, we need to be reminded the Lord created us for this divine assignment.

YOU-ARE-HERE QUESTION

Is there a place where you currently need someone to be bold with you? Are you acting like part of motherhood is optional?

It is good to have friends and family who push us toward who we were called to be. My mother spoke boldly to me because she knows the Lord, and she was confident He had chosen me to be a mother and was equipping me to be one.

Whether I felt equipped or not.

I believe my mom's boldness was passed down from her mother and has now been passed down to me. The traits we want to see in our children must first develop in us. We cannot give them something we don't have. So if I want to pass down boldness to my children as well, where do I start? Where does boldness come from?

It starts with confidence in knowing the Lord is always at work.

The traits we want to see in our children
must first develop in us.

In the book of Esther, the name of the Lord is never mentioned, yet we see His hand weaving together the details of her story. Esther's life is full of heartache, intrigue, murder plots and her bold self-sacrifice. (Go read it and see for yourself. It's definitely worth your time.)

The Lord lifted Esther up to be queen in order that she would be in a position to be bold on behalf of His people. She was in the right place at the right time. But even Esther needed a push of encouragement. Her uncle Mordecai tells her in Esther 4:14, "For if you remain silent at this time, relief and deliverance for the Jews will arise from another place, but you and your father's family will perish. And who knows but that you have come to your royal position for such a time as this?"

You are in the right place at the right time, too. We can lament the state of this world, but the Lord is not surprised by our circumstances any more than He was surprised in Esther's day. God intends that you would be a light in a dark world. Because we know our God equips His people, we can say with confidence that you are prepared for what you are now facing.

Whenever you feel inadequate, just think about what my mother said when I brought home my first baby. I was overwhelmed with exhaustion and emotion. I thought I needed sleep, but what I really needed was my mother's boldness, reminding me just as Mordecai reminded Esther: "You *can* do this, and you *will*."

 DROP-A-PIN VERSE

May He equip you with all you need for doing His will. May he produce in you, through the power of Jesus Christ, every good thing that is pleasing to Him. Hebrews 13:21 NLT

DIRECTION QUESTION

List three people in your life who have encouraged you to live boldly.

_____

_____

_____

PRAYER PROMPT

Ask the Lord to help believe that you are exactly where you are supposed to be. Thank Him for the people who inspire boldness in your life.

_____

_____

_____

I have no problem speaking my mind or letting people know how I feel. But somehow I seem to lose "my voice" or "my convictions" every time I take one of our animals to the vet. I am worried the vet and their assistants are going to think I am a fraud.

We love our animals, but we are also on a budget. When I am talking to Tony in the privacy of our own home, I am sure we do not need to spend an exorbitant amount of money on our pets. But when I am in the vet's office, it is another story.

They say, "Your turtle needs x-rays."

I say, "Of course. Whatever it takes."

The day I agreed that our guinea pig needed an IV was the day Tony decided he would attend all future vet appointments.

The truth is, I am the same at the hair salon; somehow I lose my voice. I remember one time in college, I thought I was ready for a hair adventure.

I told the stylist, "Do whatever you want. You are the professional. I trust you."

Maybe I should have grown concerned when the hairdresser said, "I am going to need to dye your eyebrows to complete the look."

It might not have been the best idea to put my complete trust in someone I didn't know. Still I smiled at my new, blond hair in the mirror and told her, "Wow. It looks great."

I want to grow in my boldness in saying no to vet expenditures, hair adventures, and to thinking I need to parent just like everyone else. My desire to please people I don't even know swallows up my boldness in these three areas.

YOU-ARE-HERE QUESTION

Is there a place in your life where you have a tendency to lose your voice? Or not speak up for your convictions?

_____

_____

_____

When I hesitate to be bold, it is because I desire to please others. Lately, I am asking the Lord to make my convictions stronger than my desire to make everyone happy ... or make everyone think I am happy.

We can encourage boldness by encouraging difference. Please do not keep assessing how well your children blend in with their surroundings. Sometimes the Lord asks each of us to stand out. Let's celebrate those moments. Holding opinions or hopes that are different than everyone else can make you feel embarrassed.

When I was growing up sometimes I would say something in public and realize I was the only one who held that particular opinion. I remember coming to my parents to say, "We are the only family who does things this way."

Secretly, I was hoping they would put their arms around me and say, "We'll change."

> *Shifting the way you think about fitting in*
> *can have a dramatic impact on the way you live,*
> *speak, and encourage others.*

Instead they would smile at us and say, "Yes! Mission accomplished. We are different." They encouraged boldness and taught me that we weren't trying to look like everyone else.

Overall, that made me more confident standing alone as an adult. Shifting the way you think about fitting in can have a dramatic impact on the way you live, speak, and encourage others.

Looking back, I can see some of my parents' values had a direct impact on me. Here are a few that encourage boldness:

- I know my parents always wanted me to be safe, but they talked to us more about being adventurous. "Be safe" wasn't something they said. "Be a leader," was what I heard most often.
- They did not talk badly about people who failed when attempting great things. Those people were talked about with admiration.

Standing out can feel scary or even isolating. It can bring up the same feeling you had at the middle school dance when you were in a huge crowd, yet felt completely alone. Jesus was with you at that moment; and He is with you now. You never stand alone.

 DROP-A-PIN VERSE

But as for me, I am filled with power, with the spirit of the Lord and with justice and might. Micah 3:8

DIRECTION QUESTION

Where do you want to grow in your boldness?

_____

_____

_____

PRAYER PROMPT

Ask the Lord to help you be bold in your prayers. Ask Him to allow you to see the size of His power and ability in your life.

_____

_____

_____

Eden wants a horse. She tries to work that thought into every single writing assignment she gets at school. Her desires are well documented. To date, Tony and I have not wavered in our response to her. We are not getting a horse.

Eden still saved up her own money and bought a horse grooming kit so she would be ready.

As her hopes continued to grow, we sat down with her again to talk about money and time. We showed her on paper the reasons why a horse is not a possibility for our family. She said she understood so when her daily prayers still included asking for a horse, I stopped her and said, "We've talked about this, Eden. You are not getting a horse."

Then, because I sometimes crush dreams, I said, "We have also told your grandparents not to buy you a horse."

She just smiled and said, "Mom, what makes it a prayer is neither of us can figure out how it would ever happen so we give it to God."

I couldn't argue with that.

Eden continued to be bold in her prayers, and I continued to shake my head until one day we ran into our neighbor. It had not been that long since we had moved into our neighborhood, and we had never noticed that at the back of their property, they kept a horse. In Texas it is not uncommon for someone with a small piece of land to own one. To our amazement, our neighbor invited Eden to take part in caring for this beautiful animal.

Our neighbor had a horse just waiting to be groomed, and we had a girl with a grooming kit.

Tony's and my jaws dropped. Eden, however, walked confidently into a story her parents had no part in writing. Her fresh faith was a shot in the arm for ours.

Praise God that He is not limited to our ability to figure out how something will work. May His glory continue to be revealed through a little girl who is loving a neighbor's horse like it's her very own. God is working everywhere.

May we all have eyes, faith, and the boldness to believe.

YOU-ARE-HERE QUESTION

Is there a place where you have held back in prayer for yourself or your family because you wanted to figure it out how it could happen first?

_____

_____

_____

Parenting boldly means believing God is writing our story, and we don't have to have all the details of how it's going to work. So much of this life is trusting the Lord to work things out. This is difficult when we are just waiting on the Lord for ourselves, but it can be even harder when we are waiting on the Lord for our children. I kept trying to stop Eden's prayer because I did not want her to be disappointed with God. I almost robbed her of seeing Him work.

Parenting boldly means believing God is writing our story, and we don't have to have all the details of how it's going to work.

You and I have to think about the messages that we are sending to our children. Teaching boldness does not require a long lesson as much as small, consistent ones. Look for opportunities to talk about the Lord:

- While in the car. (Ask the teens to put their phones down for a bit.)
- While you are changing diapers. (Tell your baby the good things God has planned for them.)
- While you are cleaning up. (Encourage your children with what you see them doing well.)
- While you are working on anything together. (Talk about how you love the heart God has placed within them.)

The Lord is always at work. When we hold tightly to that truth, it enables us to be bold in our prayers and in our lives.

 DROP-A-PIN VERSE

That is why we can say without any doubt or fear, "The Lord is my Helper, and I am not afraid of anything that mere man can do to me." Hebrews 13:6 TLB

DIRECTION QUESTION

Is there a situation where you are wanting to encourage boldness in yourself or in your family?

_____

_____

_____

PRAYER PROMPT

Ask the Lord for things that will reveal His power at work in your family.

_____

_____

_____

Eden started kindergarten on the same day Payton started middle school. I was completely prepared for the tears as I dropped off Eden. The lump in my throat when we pulled up to the middle school caught me off guard.

Were these students? How were some of these middle-schoolers already adults? To me, it looked like there were grown men with beards carrying backpacks into that building. I turned around and looked at Payton in the back seat and asked the only question I could think of, "Do you think you want to homeschool?"

I was in no way prepared to handle the difficult task of educating my child, but if he had said yes in that moment, I would've tried to figure it out. He half-smiled, shook his head, and got out of the car.

Those first few weeks were rough. Change was difficult. He missed his elementary school, where he was known by his teachers and friends. He wished he could go back to a place where he knew he was loved. I lost sleep trying to figure out a way to smooth his path, but the Lord continuously reminded me: Strength is found in climbing over obstacles not in avoiding them.

Strength is found in climbing over obstacles not in avoiding them.

Going back was not an option. The only choice was to move forward boldly and trust that somewhere, on the other side of the awkward, another group of people was going to know and love him. We continually prayed that he would see the Lord at work and that he would trust Him. We prayed that his confidence and boldness would grow. Sometimes, before boldness can grow, we first feel weak.

YOU-ARE-HERE QUESTION

How are you encouraging boldness in the face of something new in your child's life?

_____

_____

_____

No one else has the anointing to lead your family like you and your husband do. Make time to talk to God about what you are facing. He can give you insight that will not only make you bolder in your prayers, but it will encourage that quality in your child, as well.

My focus during those first few weeks of school was getting Payton into the building and making sure he was enjoying at least some of his life. That was my goal. But when I talked to the Lord about it, He reminded me that He has a bigger vision for Payton than school attendance and temporary happiness. He is growing Payton into the man he needs to be in order to fulfill his purpose.

The baby steps you see your children taking by walking into a school building by themselves, by leading a prayer at dinner, by grabbing the hand of their sibling when they need help, are seeds. Under the direction of the Lord, those seeds can grow into men and women who are bold. Parenting is more than just keeping children fed, clothed, and somewhat happy. Be bold in asking the Lord for His wisdom and insight into the children He has placed in your home. He has it in abundance.

You are not parenting on your own. You are partnering with the God of the universe.

DROP-A-PIN VERSE

So then, with this amazing hope living in us, we step out in freedom and boldness to speak the truth.

2 Corinthians 3:12 TPT

DIRECTION QUESTION

Is there a place where you have been only seeing the baby steps and missing the fact that the Lord is doing something mighty?

_____

_____

_____

PRAYER PROMPT

Ask the Lord to help you trust His ability to produce significant growth from the monotony of everyday life.

_____

_____

_____

As I have said, Eden loves horses. They bring her joy. It has worked out for her to take horseback riding lessons at a place very close to our house. While riding at full speed one day, she had her first big fall. The horse went one way, and her body went another. She tells us the whole day felt magical until she hit the ground.

The fall knocked the wind out of her. It also shook her dreams. With tears in her eyes, she confessed, "I didn't think something that I loved this much could ever hurt me."

Have you ever felt this? Have you been stunned and shocked that something that felt like a dream could turn into something that aches?

So much of life is about learning how to get back up. People will hurt our feelings. We will say or do things we wish we could take back. Relationships that we thought were lifelong turn out to have only been for a season. It is easy to spend more time wondering where we went wrong than reminding our hearts that the Lord is with us. Do not fear. Do not despair. Pain is sometimes the cost of living boldly. Pain is a part of the process.

Here is the good news: Growth follows discomfort.

My daughter is back on her horse, determined to hold onto her joy just as tight as she holds onto the reins.

YOU-ARE-HERE QUESTION

Where do you need to get back on your horse?

_____

_____

_____

It is beautiful to see the Lord in the clear-eyed joy of a person discovering their dream. But it is also beautiful to see Him in the tear-filled, determination of a person who says, "I will try again."

My mom used to tell us we needed to make a decision about who we would be in a crisis. Because the truth of the matter is, a crisis is going to come to us and our children at some point in life. Will we be people who keep going? Will we be a people who remember the Lord is with us? We have to make faith decisions before the crisis hits, because you go into a struggle with what you have. If you decide that you want to be a bold believer, then you take steps now to prepare yourself.

> *We have to make faith decisions*
> *before the crisis hits, because you go into*
> *a struggle with what you have.*

Some steps you can take to grow your boldness:

1. **Spend time in God's word.** You can't cling to promises you do not know. Make time to share with your children the scriptures that make you bold.
2. **Ask the Lord for small and mighty things.** Consider keeping a journal of the Lord's faithfulness to your family. A personal history of the Lord's faithfulness can do wonders in inspiring boldness in your child and in future generations.
3. **Take a stand for things that are right.** Talk with them about the discomfort that comes with that, as well as the strength that comes from the Lord at the same time.
4. **Tell your children that you are determined to keep your faith.** Be honest about your doubts, but also share your victories. An honest faith is a bold faith.

Your determination to be bold is seen by our God and all those who witness your life. May He bless you every step of the way.

 DROP-A-PIN VERSE

Guilty criminals experience paranoia even though no one threatens them. But the innocent lovers of God, because of righteousness, will have the boldness of a young, ferocious lion!

Proverbs 28:1 TPT

DIRECTION QUESTION

What action steps do you want to take this week to be bold in your life and in your family?

_____

_____

_____

PRAYER PROMPT

Ask the Lord to give you the boldness of a young, ferocious lion. Ask Him to show you where He is calling you to stand strong.

_____

_____

_____

When You're Overwhelmed

Like most kids her age, Shelby doesn't like storms. The combination of thunder and lightning overwhelm her. Once when she was three, we were trying to assure her that all would be fine, and 6-year-old Eden said, "Shelby, you are forgetting what God told you when you were born. You have to remember."

I asked, "Eden, what did God tell Shelby?"

"The same thing He tells every baby. He says, 'There are going to be some hard and scary things in this world, but you know Me, and I love you. I am with you. Don't forget you know Me.'"

Powerful, precious words. It was sweet seeing Shelby listen to them, stop crying, and go to sleep.

It would be easy to just tell you that part of the story and have you think our family is always having spiritual moments like this.

Wait, there's more. Just as we were really soaking up the sweetness of the thoughts Eden had just shared, Payton quipped, "I doubt that ever happened."

We quickly gave him the *Stop-talking-right-now* look.

Then we turned back to Eden and said, "What you just shared with Shelby sounds like our God, and it matches up with the truth we know. Hold onto that. He loves you and is with you."

There is peace and power in remembering. The Lord is gentle with us all. Isaiah 40:11 says "He tends his flock like a shepherd: He gathers the lambs in his arms and carries them close to His heart; He gently leads those who have young." God hasn't changed since the days of Isaiah. He still longs to gently gather you and carry you close to His heart.

In the middle of the storm, don't forget you know Him.

YOU-ARE-HERE QUESTION

Has there been a time when remembering the Lord calmed the storm in your heart?

_____

_____

_____

In 1 Kings 19:1, We meet up with God's prophet Elijah. Elijah has just lived through an incredible day with the Lord. In the previous chapter, the people of Israel have witnessed God defeat the prophets of Baal in spectacular fashion. (Please read this wonderful story for yourself.)

Because he has just lived through such a powerful experience, we are a bit shocked to see how Elijah begins doubting himself. He is walking into the storm. How quickly people can move from joy to despair.

> Satan knows one of his best targets
> is a tired person questioning themselves.

In my own life, the birth of my first child was one of the best moments I'd ever experienced, and doubt and despair followed closely behind. Have you ever experienced a moment more powerful than when your child was placed in your arms? Whether they came from your womb, adoption, or foster care, you know the Lord's power shone forth in mighty ways when that child came into your home, but you will still experience discouragement at times. If it happened to one of the Lord's best prophets we should not be thrown off when it happens to us. The enemy always shows up after a victory. Satan knows one of his best targets is a tired person questioning himself.

Elijah gets tired and overwhelmed and after all his mighty prayers the day before, all he can eke out in his next prayer is: "Go ahead and kill me."

> *The Lord's directives for his servants*
> *don't sound like a general,*
> *they sound like a gentle father.*

I love that scripture gives us this honest portrayal of this mighty man. It might be easy to imagine a God who would say, "I have done so many great things for you, and this is how you act? Get up."

That is far from what the Lord does.

The Lord's directives for his servants don't sound like a general, they sound like a gentle father:

1. You need to rest.
2. You need to eat.

When you start feeling the signs and seeing the signals of discouragement, remember how the Lord took care of Elijah. He wants to take care of you in the same way. Take a moment to do a self check. Have you eaten food that nourishes your body? What is your sleep like? Acknowledge the Lord in these things. He cares for you just as he cared for His prophet. Sometimes we can get so caught up in the big things of God and family that we forget God is honored in small things.

Rest. Eat. Remember the Lord.

DROP-A-PIN VERSE

Let us acknowledge the Lord; let us press on to acknowledge him.
As surely as the sun rises, he will appear; he will come to us like
the winter rains, like the spring rains that water the earth.

Hosea 6:3

DIRECTION QUESTION

Where could you take better care of yourself?

_____

_____

_____

PRAYER PROMPT

Ask the Lord to remind you that sometimes the best thing you
can do for the Kingdom is rest. Ask for His strength to follow
through.

_____

_____

_____

Questions flooded my mind as soon as my first child was born. I didn't know who to turn to for answers. Everyone had a different opinion on everything. Some friends told me I was on antibiotics too long during childbirth. Some friends talked to me about nursing or formula or co-sleeping or crying it out or ... the list kept going.

It was not that anyone was trying to apply pressure, it was that I was already questioning myself. Was I stimulating my baby's mind too much? Too little? Never had I wanted to do something more right. But I was so tired. I cried a lot. I loved our baby, and I also was convinced that I was in over my head. I knew the Lord had a plan, but I could not imagine how I could be a player in it.

One night I woke up and could not find our infant anywhere. I was terrified and quickly went and got Tony. I remember seeing fear in his eyes and thinking, "Tony is terrified, too! Where is our baby?!"

With that concerned expression still on his face, he reached for me and said, "You are holding him, Becky. I am going to take him from you now."

That is tired.

That is a mind temporarily absent. I was overwhelmed with this new responsibility of caring for a child. I knew I had to find an anchor that would hold in the deep waters of motherhood.

My anchor came in knowing the Lord and His word. I had to learn anew that God was for me in motherhood just as He had been for every mother in the history of mankind. Prayer helped me to become aware of moments when I could be sleeping instead of choosing something of lesser value. I had to learn to put down my phone, the remote, the book I was enjoying, and close my eyes.

Psalm 16:7 tells us, "I will praise the Lord who counsels me, even at night, my heart instructs me." Sometimes the best cure for the overwhelmed heart is sleep. He created rest to restore your body and minister to your mind.

YOU-ARE-HERE QUESTION

Has there been a point in motherhood where you were completely overwhelmed and did something crazy? Hopefully it's something you can laugh about now ...

_____

_____

_____

Elijah is tired. As he questions himself, the Lord sends an angelic messenger who touches him and says, "Get up and eat, for the journey is too much for you."

What a gift these words are to us. The Lord recognizes that often it is "too much." The Lord then asks Elijah, "What are you doing here?"

Elijah repeats the same phrase _twice_ when the Lord asks him what is going on. He says, "I have been very zealous for the Lord God Almighty. The Israelites have rejected your covenant, torn down your altars, and put your prophets to death with your sword. I am the only one left, and now they are trying to kill me, too" (1 Kings 19:10).

When you are overwhelmed, the enemy of your soul will whisper a repeating thought to you. Seeing this happen to Elijah helps us remember the enemy's tactics have not changed. Decide now where you want your thoughts to go during stress.

Elijah had a negative thought on repeat in his head. Many times, I have done that as well. The Lord helps bring Elijah out of this negative spiral. He can use worship and scripture to bring us out of ours as well. Do you have a favorite scripture or song that you can turn to immediately? We can learn a lot about the enemy's tactics through watching Elijah. We can also create tactics of our own.

I love the way the Lord brings Elijah back to right thinking. He says, "Go out and stand on the mountain in the presence of the Lord, for the Lord is about to pass by" (verse 11). Sometimes we need to go outside. We need to watch the sunrise or the leaves fall. We need to get some perspective on the Lord's power. Quiet your heart and listen for the gentle whisper of God. It reassured Elijah that he was not alone, and it can reassure us as well.

DROP-A-PIN VERSE

You will keep them in perfect peace, whose mind is fixed on you, because they trust in you.　　　　　Isaiah 26:3 NLT

DIRECTION QUESTION

Where are you needing the Lord's perspective on you or your family?

_____

_____

_____

PRAYER PROMPT

Ask the Lord to help you center your mind on Him. As you take deep breaths, exhale your stress and inhale His power. Ask Him to help you see Him at work in the world around you so that your confidence in Him will grow.

_____

_____

_____

I have a cherished picture of our girls sitting together with their arms around each other watching the sunset. If you don't know the story behind the picture, you would assume that these are two siblings who adore each other. You would be right, but that still wouldn't give you the whole picture.

You see, in the minutes before this beautiful moment, Shelby forgot to shut the rabbit cage. We have three rabbits, and they are fast. Unfortunately our neighbor's dog is faster. When the rabbits escape, everyone goes into full panic mode trying to save them before they are eaten. We run like maniacs, and the rabbits think we are playing some silly game. They dart and dash while we try to save them.

In stressful moments like that, it is easy to lose control. Some people get loud. Some people get angry. Some people say things they don't mean.

When our mouths get loud, it is a red flag
that it's time for our hearts to get quiet.

What does chasing rabbits have to do with that lovely sunset picture of two sisters holding each other? That gentle hug was Eden's way of saying, "The rabbits are safe now, and I'm sorry I said, 'You'll pay for this.'"

Have you ever had a *You'll-pay-for-this* moment with someone? It is a moment when your heart is racing, your neck is tight, and you want a resolution. When our mouths get loud, it is a red flag that it's time for our hearts to get quiet. It would help to remember the Lord has never said, "You'll pay for this."

Instead He asked Jesus to die for our sin. *He* paid for it.

So the next time the enemy tempts you to say, "You'll pay for this," remember Jesus already did.

YOU-ARE-HERE QUESTION

When was the last time you were loud in a stressful moment?

_____

_____

_____

Every now and then, children need a time-out. Sometimes parents need one, as well. The Lord spoke, and the world came into existence with His breath. He certainly knows how to breathe life. So take a step back and ask Him to breathe life into you. Be truthful with your children in times of stress, saying, "Mom needs a minute." That's a phrase I use often.

In childbirth class they always remind you to get a focal point. If you can focus, you can manage the pain. Life can feel a lot like labor, so find your focal point and fix your eyes on Jesus.

Families who are fixed on Jesus know what helps them keep their vision and what causes them to get distracted. Healthy families have communication boundaries and household routines in order to keep their focus. It is important to know our limits and know when we are pushing our children and ourselves too much. If our homes are filled with constant complaining, rushing, and *You'll-pay-for-this* moments, it is time to set some new boundaries and routines. Ask the Lord for clarity.

While it is helpful to create boundaries and routines, please remain flexible. There will be unexpected interruptions to the routines of the day, and I have learned to trust that it is the Lord directing me. The dishes may not always be clean, and the to-do list may not always have check marks on it, but I don't want to be so consumed with my routines that I miss the one the Lord has set for me. I am learning to relax in the Lord's hand, which in turn helps me relax in my own home. God has a plan for who you are as a family. Take a time-out and ask Him to show you His ways.

 ## DROP-A-PIN VERSE

Don't worry about anything; instead pray about everything; tell God your needs, and don't forget to thank him for his answers. If you do this, you will experience God's peace, which is far more wonderful than the human mind can understand. His peace will keep your heart quiet and at rest as you trust in Jesus.

Philippians 4:6-7 TLB

DIRECTION QUESTION

Is there a place in your life where you have resisted the Lord's direction for your day?

_____

_____

_____

PRAYER PROMPT

Thank God for the ways you see Him at work.

_____

_____

_____

When our two boys were in elementary, Picture Day was just like every other day of the school year. The night before I would usually suggest, "Why don't you wear a shirt with a collar?"

Sometimes they nodded and did exactly that, sometimes they opted for a different look, but it was a day without much fanfare.

For my girls, it was the exact opposite. Picture Day still brings with it a great amount of stress for them. We can't get up early enough. For years, as our Picture Day mornings dissolved into tears, I would wonder what had happened. Then it dawned on me: They have a vision in their heads of what they are supposed to look like on Picture Day, and we are not achieving their vision. On most days, a t-shirt, jeans, and a pony tail feels right, but on Picture Day they want to be transformed. Oh, what I wouldn't give to have a cosmetologist's skills so I could help them achieve their vision.

On one particular Picture Day morning, I could not get Shelby's naturally curly hair to do what she wanted. According to her, I was brushing it too hard. Then, I was not straightening it fast enough. Then she was upset because there was still a hint of a wave when we pulled it back. I felt my neck getting tight with stress because I wanted to get her to school on time. I was doing my best, but she was still frustrated because it didn't look right. I did not know what "right" looked like. She started to cry.

I wish I had felt overwhelmed with grace and mercy for Shelby. Instead, I felt overwhelmed with anger at her. I told her we had to stop, her hair looked fine, and it was time to get in the car. Her silent tears fell the whole way to school. As I drove, my mind was racing with thoughts like, *She should appreciate that I was trying. She should like her curly hair.*

Then those thoughts shifted with this lightning-fast progression:

Other moms don't have problems like this.
You are the worst at doing your daughters' hair.
You should watch more YouTube videos on braids, on straightening, on styling.
You aren't even that great with your own hair.
You should be a better mom.
You are failing.

By the time we were in the drop off line in front of the school, both Shelby and I were sad. Usually we exchange smiles and I-love-yous before she gets out of the car. This morning, the only sound was silence and a slamming door. As I pulled away my tears started to fall. What a mess of a morning. I drove a few blocks and then pulled over to the side of the residential street and began to pray. I confessed my frustration with Shelby. I confessed my anger that she was frustrated with me. I confessed how I felt like an untalented mom who wrestles with styling her own hair, let alone her daughters' hair. I confessed I was completely overwhelmed with Picture Day and the havoc it had brought to our usually pleasant morning. I confessed that just as Shelby had a vision in her mind of how her hair should look, I had a vision in my mind of how a good mom should look. Shelby felt frustration over her vision for hair. I felt frustration over my vision for motherhood. Neither of us matched the picture we wanted. As I confessed all of it to the Lord, I felt Him lead my heart to grace and mercy.

He gave it to me so that I could give it to Shelby.

I turned my car around and went back to the school. I went into the office and asked if I could see Shelby for a brief conversation. As soon as I saw her walking down the hall, my heart flooded with love. I pulled her close and whispered, "I didn't like who I was this morning. I could have handled everything better. I still think your hair is beautiful. Will you forgive me?"

She said she forgave me, and for the first time that morning, gave me a big smile.

It was picture perfect.

God can take our sad silences and slamming doors and turn them into smiles and hugs in hallways. We may not look like the vision we had in our minds, but with God's grace and mercy, our overwhelmed hearts can become transformed hearts. He is a redeeming God, able to redeem our lives.

Even on Picture Day.

On that memorable morning, I forgot that Shelby and I are a team. We are both learning to have patience in dealing with her hair. It's always good to teach a lesson about patience. But sometimes the best lesson I could teach is: "You can't even imagine how much I love you."

YOU-ARE-HERE QUESTION

Is there a moment you felt overwhelmed that you need God to redeem?

_____

_____

_____

On the night Jesus was arrested to be crucified, His disciples were overwhelmed. Here was the man and leader they loved being arrested for a crime they knew he did not commit. Their confusion is completely understandable. I wonder if they were stunned that their vision for themselves and for Jesus looked nothing like what was really happening.

I am so glad one of the first things Jesus did when He rose was go and tell those same men—who had so quickly gone from confident friends of Jesus to men trying to hide that they knew Him—that they were still His first choice in spreading the good news of the Kingdom.

> *Grace and mercy changed Jesus' disciples,*
> *and they are still changing us.*

When you make mistakes in your parenting the enemy will try to convince you that you have thrown off the Lord's plan. Be confident that you have not. Let your overwhelmed heart be transformed by the overwhelming love of Jesus. Our God can take disciples who once denied Jesus and transform them into men who change the world holding His name high. That same God can take a discouraged mom and transform her into a mom who puts courage into the hearts of her children.

Grace and mercy changed Jesus' disciples, and they are still changing us.

 DROP-A-PIN VERSE

I will be your God throughout your lifetime. I made you, and I will care for you. I will carry you along and save you.

Isaiah 46:4 NLT

DIRECTION QUESTION

Where in your life do you need to let grace and mercy transform you?

_____

_____

_____

PRAYER PROMPT

Ask the Lord to remind you that you are His first choice to mother your children. Ask Him to help you receive His grace and mercy so you can give it to them.

_____

_____

_____

Thoughts from 7-year-old Shelby:

"Last night I had something on my mind that made me feel overwhelmed. I knew I wouldn't be able to sleep until I figured it out. So I just lay there thinking for a long time …

Then my heart heard, *Shelby, you have eight-and-a-half years before you need to know what you want on your personalized license plates.*

So I smiled and said, 'Lord, you're never wrong,' and I went to sleep."

Personalized license plates were keeping her up at night. Isn't it interesting what can make people feel overwhelmed? Today I am praying that we will trust the voice of the Lord with the faith of a 7-year-old.

Exodus 14:14 tells us, "The Lord will fight for you; you need only be still."

May we learn to say, "Lord, you're never wrong," and be at peace.

YOU-ARE-HERE QUESTION

How are you at being still and trusting?

_____

_____

_____

One night Payton came out of his room and said, "I signed you up to bring breakfast tomorrow morning to my science class.

I immediately looked at him and said, "Breakfast tomorrow? It's 10 o'clock!"

He nodded and smiled.

Here's the backstory. Earlier in the week, I had been thinking about what overwhelms me most. It is when I am caught off guard by something. In that situation, I have a tendency to become a mean version of myself. Because I am wanting to change that, I had written the words "Calm and Kind" and put them in several places where I would see them regularly. There was one in my car, one on my bathroom mirror, and one behind the kitchen sink.

It just so happened that as Payton came out of his room, I was standing at the sink taking care of our dinner dishes. As soon as I said, "It's 10 o'clock!" that little note caught my eye, and I took a deep breath. The time to bring about change in your child is not in the middle of the stressful situation. Children are rarely taught something new in their moment of need.

I held off on my anger and told Payton I would drive him to the store, but he would go in and get the breakfast supplies on his own. I decided to address the timing of his communication about school later. Yes, he needed to know that 10 p.m. was too late to tell me about a class breakfast for the next morning, but he didn't need the instruction right then. At the moment, he was consumed with thoughts about not letting down his whole science class, and he wouldn't have heard a word.

Save your lesson for a time when your child can listen.

On the way to the store, we were making casual conversation. Then with a sincere tone of gratitude, Payton said, "When no one else signed up to bring things for breakfast, I told my teacher you would handle it because you love thinking of others."

Wait. What? Did the Lord just hand me a blessing from my son, right in the middle of my frustration?

He did. And I am so glad I was not in the middle of a lecture, or I would have missed it.

Here's the truth I want you to hold onto. If you are not overwhelmed at this moment, you will be overwhelmed in the future. Decide now who you want to be in that moment. Being overwhelmed will temporarily blind you to the blessings of God. Hold firmly to the knowledge that there is more to life than what you can see in the moment. Honor God's vision of you so you don't lose sight of what is important.

> *Being overwhelmed will temporarily*
> *blind you to the blessings of God.*

 ## DROP-A-PIN VERSE

I remain confident of this: I will see the goodness of the Lord in the land of the living. Wait for the Lord; be strong and take heart and wait for the Lord.　　　　Psalm 27:13-14

DIRECTION QUESTION

Where do you want to see the goodness of the Lord?

_____

_____

_____

PRAYER PROMPT

Ask the Lord to help you see His goodness right here in the land of the living. Ask Him to encourage you as you wait for Him.

How Discipline
Works

My dad is 6'7." The builder installed all of the bathroom mirrors in my childhood home at average height Those mirrors worked for everyone but my dad. He had to squat to look at his hair as he combed it.

One day, we noticed my younger brother Sam was squatting as he combed his hair. Sam could see himself in the mirror, even when he was standing up straight, but that made no difference. He had watched our dad squat while he combed his hair, and Sam thought that was the natural position of a man who needed to comb his hair. My dad had unknowingly discipled my brother in this area.

YOU-ARE-HERE QUESTION

What is one thing you do that has no other explanation other than, "That's what my parents did?"

_____

_____

_____

So many traits are caught rather than taught. We become like those we hang around, and for the first 18 years of our lives, we are hanging around our parents more than anyone else. Children are being shaped from the very beginning of life by what they watch their parents do. The Lord will open many doors through which one can walk through in order to know Jesus better. The first door He often offers is a child's parents.

Parents are accomplishing a lot when they discipline their children. The root word of *discipline* is *disciple*. I don't know why that has not stood out to me before. As we parent with discipling in mind, many things become clear. Jesus walked with His disciples, he worked with His disciples, he modeled life for His disciples. He trained them by letting them watch Him. That is what we are supposed to be doing with our children. When we think of the word *discipline*, we tend to think of correction. Sure, discipline used as a verb can mean to punish or rebuke, but discipline used as a noun can mean a lifetime practice.

Oh Jesus, show us how to walk in discipline.

Discipline is of great value. It requires knowing yourself and knowing your child. It will always be easier to buy every child a device or let them watch TV than it is to discipline them. Our electronics produce a form of synthetic discipline. Our children are quiet, they are in control of themselves, and parents are able to get things done. Children appear well-behaved. But remove the electronics, and what once looked like discipline is gone.

> *Our electronics produce a form of synthetic discipline.*

The life of a person who is abiding in Christ is not synthetic, it is organic. In the same way that organic produce is the more expensive option in a grocery store, the spiritual fruit that comes from an organic relationship with Jesus is valuable. Everything about it is real, even the discipline. There is nothing synthetic about abiding in Christ. It takes work. You have to tend to it daily. Love, joy, peace, patience, kindness, goodness, faithfulness, gentleness, and self-control are the "organic produce" of a life of discipline. They are products of the Holy Spirit, often revealed to a child through the lives of his or her parents.

It's important to remember that none of us are raising Jesus, and none of us *are* Jesus. There are going to be mistakes. None of us will be able to raise a child who is all things to all people, but through discipline, we can bring our children closer to Jesus. We do this by asking ourselves, "Are the qualities that I want to see in my children currently being produced in me?"

Before we talk about working in the fertile soil of our children's hearts, we have to acknowledge there's work to be done in our own hearts. Look at the fruit your life is producing. Would it bless your children to pattern their lives after yours?

The Lord is able to do great things with whatever you give Him. When I am using the map app on my phone, and I take a wrong turn, the app has never told me, "You'll never get there now. You can't recover from this mistake."

No, map apps are designed to continue to work in spite of human error. They take a few seconds to get their location, and then they give us one of my favorite words: "Re-routing."

Your mistakes or wrong turns are just re-routing. The Lord can work through all of them to disciple you and your children. Job 42:2 says, "I know that you [God] can do anything, and no one can stop you" (NLT). What comfort this can bring! Our faults cannot throw off the will of God.

He will prevail, and—no matter how many times we re-route—we will reach His intended destination.

 DROP-A-PIN VERSE

I am the Lord and I will not share my glory with another.

Isaiah 42:8

DIRECTION QUESTION

Where are you needing to re-route?

_____

_____

_____

PRAYER PROMPT

Ask the Lord to help you see your own heart. Ask Him to lead you in the disciplining of yourself, as well as your children.

_____

_____

_____

When Shelby was a toddler, she grabbed my arm while I was holding a hot cup of coffee. I nearly spilled it on myself and on her. My reaction was strong. The tone in my voice reflected concern and irritation when I said, "I'm holding something hot, why would you grab my arm?"

When I stopped reacting long enough to study my sweet girl's face, I saw a mixture of confusion and fear. That is when I realized she might not have known what she was doing. I had not intentionally taught her that coffee cups contain something hot. So, for the first time I showed her the difference between cups people drink hot drinks out of and those used for cold drinks. We talked about looking to see what someone is holding before we grab their arm. What had started off as a scalding had turned into a scolding. But then it had turned again into a sweet conversation for both of us.

YOU-ARE-HERE QUESTION

Have you ever gotten frustrated with your child for not knowing something, only to realize you had not yet taught it to them?

_____

_____

_____

Often children do something wrong because they have not been taught to do something right. It's so easy to create doubt and insecurity in our children by coming at them with an attitude of, "You should know this by now."

Should they know this by now?

Discipline means coming alongside our children. It means working shoulder to shoulder. It means saying, "We're in this together and you are important." It means reaching out to our children just as our Savior Jesus Christ has so wonderfully reached out to us. He extends us grace so we can extend it to those around us. Our time with our children is a short 18 years. Thankfully, we have our Jesus to help us make the most of it. As we teach our children to walk alongside us, we are also teaching them to walk alongside Him.

> *Often children do something wrong because they have not been taught to do something right.*

We want our children to look like Jesus. We want them to come with us in serving and honoring our God. But in order for that to happen, we have to train them. Just as Jesus chose a group of men to walk with, He has chosen your family for you. Think of it: at the end of Jesus' life, His disciples knew what He stood for. They were confident of His beliefs. He had trained them. He knew their strengths, and He knew their weaknesses. Jesus' disciples knew him well, but they also knew they were a part of something bigger than themselves.

These days, families need that same reminder. We have a banner that hangs in our garage that reads, "Team Brooks." We see it every day. It's a reminder that the Lord placed us on the same team for a reason. We are for each other.

How can we discipline our children with a heart to disciple them? Here's one of the most powerful questions I ask myself: Are my expectations clear?

- Your children cannot read your mind.
- Get in the habit of using the car ride to go over how your family acts in whatever situation you are about to enter.
- Talk about the expectations for your team every day. (Such as, *We are kind. We look for people who might need help. We smile. We are respectful.*)
- Explain to them the "why" behind what you do.

Character training happens on a daily basis. All day long, you are teaching what is appropriate, and what is not. Intentionally talk about the characteristics you want to see in your child and let them see those characteristics in you.

DIRECTION QUESTION

In what area are you committing to discipling your child this week?

_____

_____

_____

PRAYER PROMPT

Ask the Lord to help you clarify your expectations. Ask Him to give you strength and energy to disciple as Jesus did.

_____

_____

_____

I have mentioned that both our boys had injuries that required casts in the same year. Well, there was one more. Yes, three out of four children were in casts during the same twelve-month period.

Shelby got a deep bone bruise underneath her knee cap from falling while we were hiking. Her knee kept swelling so her doctor recommended she be on crutches for a few days. She did well with this inconvenience until the very last day. As she was limping down the hall, one of her crutches landed on a piece of paper. The crutch slipped out from under her, and she fell hard.

I could not believe it when she told me through tears, "I think I just broke my arm."

We met with our orthopedist who confirmed Shelby's suspicions. She needed a cast. Immediately I started thinking of Benjamin, who had only recently had his two casts removed. The arm in a short cast below his elbow required almost no rehab, but the arm in a full cast up to his armpit required rehab to regain normal movement. I did not want that for Shelby.

Truthfully, I did not want that for *me*.

When our doctor said, "Shelby is going to need a full arm cast."

I quickly said, "No. We would like to do a short one."

Our doctor is gracious, and he looked at me with kind eyes. His tone was clear when he said, "I know you are tired of this process. I know this is your third child to be here getting a cast. But for Shelby's wrist to heal correctly, she needs a full arm cast. So that's what we are going to do."

I knew he was right. Despite the discomfort and inconvenience, I wanted full healing for Shelby. Her arm needed that full cast.

When was the last time the Lord healed you through discomfort and inconvenience?

_____

_____

_____

My exhaustion with having a child in a cast didn't get to change Shelby's healing plan. My exhaustion also does not get to change the Lord's healing plans for me. I texted a few friends a picture of Shelby in her cast with the words, "The Lord must be trying to teach me something that I have yet to learn."

I cried as I typed that. As sure as Shelby's arm needed a cast to discipline that bone and mold it into the right shape, my heart needs the discipline of the Lord to mold me as well. The doctor was the expert on bones. The Lord is the expert on life.

If I could have, I would have shielded my children from pain at every opportunity. That's what a mom does. But this time last year we were praying as a family that the Lord would take us deeper in our friendships, that He would grow in us a heart of compassion, and that we would find our identity in Christ alone.

And guess what? The Year of Casts has been producing everything we prayed for. Our children have friends they know on a whole new level because they had to ask for help. They have a heart for the hurting because they've felt hurt themselves. They have had to find out who they were apart from their extra-curricular activities. They have asked hard questions and seen the Lord answer.

My attempts to shield my children from pain would have kept them from the blessings God intended to give within it.

> *Every time He takes something away,*
> *He gives something else.*

So while I hope we don't meet our deductible this year, I'm going to keep praying that our family will continue to believe that joy is not the only place Jesus is found. He is there when your bones are broken and when your heart aches. Perhaps He feels even closer during those times because we are so desperate for Him.

Remember to look for the hidden blessing in your family's painful seasons.

Every time He takes something away, He gives something else.

DROP-A-PIN VERSE

For the moment all discipline seems painful rather than pleasant, but later it yields the peaceful fruit of righteousness to those who have been trained by it. Hebrews 12:11 ESV

DIRECTION QUESTION

Is there a place in your life or in the life of someone you love where you can see "the peaceful fruit of righteousness" from having been trained by discipline?

_____

_____

_____

PRAYER PROMPT

Ask the Lord that whatever discomfort or inconvenience you are feeling will not be wasted. Ask Him to strengthen your heart.

_____

_____

_____

Going to the grocery store was always an adventure when my children were young. One time we knocked over a display in the produce section. Another time, Benjamin hid in the freezer case with his tiny face pressed up against the glass. Bringing them along was inconvenient, to say the least.

Shopping with three small children was hard enough. After we had Shelby, I decided "Four at the Grocery Store" was a game I didn't want to play. I chose to shop for groceries when Tony was available to keep our kids. I felt more confident about the use of my time if I knew all four children were home and safe with their dad. Everything went faster when I was by myself.

We continued that way for a long time, but one day I felt a surge of courage. I was going shopping with all four of them. I talked to them on the way to the store and went over my expectations. When we got there, I pushed a basket, and so did Payton. We maneuvered down the aisles much slower than I do when I am by myself.

I decided to be okay with the speed. That's when I started noticing that involvement was the key. As long as I was teaching and inviting my children into the process of shopping, they were learning and on task. When speed and convenience were no longer the goals, disciplining and discipling came easier. My day at the grocery store revealed a deeper truth about parenting. Growth is a process that's neither fast nor easy.

When you read the stories of Jesus and His twelve apostles, it seems there were times it would have been easier on Jesus to have left them at home. But His goal was not speed or convenience, it was discipleship. As a mom I have to remember that's my goal as well.

YOU-ARE-HERE QUESTION

Is there an area where you have been focused on speed and convenience instead of discipline?

_____

_____

_____

I still choose to do certain things out of speed and convenience, but I have had to realize that growth and development are not a drive-through experience. Jesus lived with His disciples, and as He did, He taught them. By living together and teaching at the same time, He was investing in His relationship with them.

My goal as a mom is to have a child who knows and loves Jesus. I also want my children to know and love me. Why? Because the Lord in His goodness gave us to each other. We are an integral part of each other's stories. My love for my children was immediate, but learning their hearts will take a lifetime.

Jesus only had three years to pour life and truth into His disciples. How sweet of the Lord to give us 18 years. What traits are you wanting to see in your children? What adventures will help you reach these goals? A trip to the grocery store can be about more than just groceries.

Fabulous growth opportunities are disguised as obligations. Sometimes a growing parent/child relationship looks like a fun trip to the zoo. Other times it looks like folding clothes or unloading the dishwasher together. Jesus knew the key to discipling was togetherness. May the Lord give us the strength to hold onto that truth as well. Doing certain things together can be exhausting, but the Lord can give us a vision for our family transforms the exhausting to the exhilarating.

Fabulous growth opportunities
are disguised as obligations.

 ## DROP-A-PIN VERSE

Start children off on the way they should go, and even when they are old they will not turn from it.   Proverbs 22:6

DIRECTION QUESTION

Is there a place where you could invite your child into your daily activities in order to give them small opportunities to grow?

_____

_____

_____

PRAYER PROMPT

Ask the Lord to disciple you in His love. Thank Him for all the times He has invited you to do things together with Him.

_____

_____

_____

When Benjamin was tiny I would try to get up early in the morning to have some time alone. I wanted time to talk to God. Usually, Benjamin was up at the same time, wanting time to talk to me. It felt as if I could not win.

Discouragement doesn't come to those on the wrong path. It comes to those on the right one. Keep reaching out for Jesus. This life, this day, isn't about winning. It's about holding on to the One who already has won. His name is Jesus

What used to cause tears, I now embrace. We are both early risers. Eventually, Benjamin matured enough to come downstairs early and, with a smile, go quietly about his business. We started sharing the morning hours I had wanted so badly to experience alone. We are alone yet together, and I treasure it. Someday I'll have my early mornings by myself again. But, this season of life is about sharing.

> *Discouragement doesn't come to those on the wrong path. It comes to those on the right one.*

Luke 6:38 reminds us, "Give generously and generous gifts will be given back to you, shaken down to make room for more. Abundant gifts will pour upon you with such an overflowing measure that it will run over the top! Your measurement of generosity becomes the measurement of your return" (TPT). One of the most generous gifts we can give to our children is time.

God can give it back to us.

YOU-ARE-HERE QUESTION

Is there a place in your life where discouragement has made you think you are on the wrong path when it might be an affirmation that you are the right one?

_____

_____

_____

Now I am thankful that my children are early risers. I had to ask the Lord for wisdom in order to appreciate what irritated me. For years I told my children, "Go back to bed." Then I realized I was not supposed to change this quality in them. I was supposed to bring it under the discipline of Christ. Some of your children's best qualities are disguised as irritations in their early years. Is what you are struggling with in your child something that needs to be corrected, or is it a quality that needs to be discipled?

This makes me think of the story in Matthew 14:22-3, when Jesus calls to Peter and invites him to walk on water. As long as Peter's eyes are on Jesus, he does well, but when he takes his eyes off Jesus, he notices the wind and waves. That's when he sinks.

What saves Peter from drowning? He reaches for the One who can pull him out of the water.

Jesus can pull you out as well. He has called you to motherhood. There will be frightening moments, as you look at the wind and the waves, but there also will be moments when you are able to lock eyes with Jesus and do hard things.

Our Savior has not changed. He stands ready to save people when they are sinking. Peter's faith didn't need to be corrected. It needed to be discipled. Peter is well known for his impulsivity, but that impulsivity, when brought under the control of God, would bring thousands to know Jesus. What seemed like an irritation was a mighty tool for the Kingdom. Praise God for a Savior like ours. He loves us as we are but will not leave us that way.

DROP-A-PIN VERSE

So here is what I want you to do, God helping you: Take your everyday, ordinary life—your sleeping, eating, going-to-work, and walking around life—and place it before God as an offering. Embracing what God does for you is the best thing you can do for Him. Don't become so well-adjusted to your culture that you fit into it without even thinking. Instead, fix your attention on God, you'll be changed from the inside out. Readily recognize what He wants from you, and quickly respond to it. Unlike the culture around you, always dragging you down to its level of immaturity, God brings out the best in you, He develops well-formed maturity in you. Romans 12: 1-2 MSG

DIRECTION QUESTION

Where do you see the Lord working to bring out the best in you?

_____

_____

_____

PRAYER PROMPT

Ask the Lord to disciple your heart in news ways. Ask Him to help you discern where what you have been viewing as irritations in yourself and in your children might actually be strengths in need of discipling.

_____

_____

_____

How to Speak Life

Once a child who is dear to my heart told me a story about something that happened at school. The child had been called "lazy" for not finishing work in class. I love this child so much that I stewed on it all night long, trying to figure out a way to confront the adult who had said it. I asked the Lord to show me the way to bring change. I was expecting that He would give me guidance so that I could say something significant to this person who was so clearly in the wrong.

I wasn't expecting the Spirit to gently remind me that the shortcomings I'm so eager to confront in others are the shortcomings I avoid facing in my own heart. Instead of pondering someone else's life throughout the night, I should have been reflecting on my own. I'm guilty and need the Lord's help in the area of words. I often speak carelessly. I want to remember the power of words. Words either heal or wound, encourage or dishearten, bless or curse. I want my words to build not tear down. I want to be one who speaks life and blessing.

Hold me to it, friends.

YOU-ARE-HERE QUESTION

Has anyone said something unkind to you that was hard to let go?

_____

_____

_____

Words have power. In Deuteronomy 30:19, The Lord asks His people to make a decision, saying, "Today, I have given you the choice between life and death, between blessings and curses. Now

I call on heaven and earth to witness the choice that you make. Oh, that you would choose life, so that you and your descendants might live" (NLT).

We want our families to choose to bless instead of condemn. We want them to choose to encourage instead of discourage. So, as mothers, wives, and children of God who have chosen "life," how do we learn to speak it over our families? How do we learn to speak it over ourselves?

First, we acknowledge our need for the Lord. If we are to become speakers of life, our hearts have to spend time with the Giver of Life. The place to start in learning to be a life-giving speaker is with my thoughts. If my mind is a parade of negativity about myself, that is going to be what comes out of my mouth. If it is difficult for us to speak life over ourselves, it will be difficult for us to speak it over others.

Satan is the one who brings up our guilt, shame, and past mistakes. Do not listen to him. Jesus brings conviction and the power to change. Listen to His voice; He does not berate or badger His children. Someone who constantly beats herself down is listening to Satan, the deceiver. Our Lord wants to affirm you so that you can affirm others. Spend as much time as you can, tuning into His voice.

If we are to become speakers of life, our hearts have to spend time with the Giver of Life.

Jesus was in tune with His Father. As a result, Jesus had much encouragement to give others. As He walked through life, His eyes were always open to see and call forth the best in those around Him. In order to speak life, we have to learn to see it.

DROP-A-PIN VERSE

And Jesus knew their thoughts, and said to them, "Every kingdom divided against itself is brought to desolation; and every city or house divided against itself, shall not stand.   Matthew 12:25

DIRECTION QUESTION

When you have time to think, do your thoughts go to a place that encourages you or discourages you?

_____

_____

_____

PRAYER PROMPT

Ask the Lord to help you rework your thoughts. Ask Him to help you be a person who sees life and calls it out in yourself and in others.

_____

_____

_____

When he was in kindergarten, Benjamin brought home a folder every day that reported on his school life. We all delighted in his work, and on occasion there was a short note from the teacher detailing something about his behavior in class.

One day it read, "Please remind Benjamin to treat others the way he wants to be treated."

I sat down to remind him that we have been working on the Golden Rule since birth.

He looked at me with a precious smile and sparkling blue eyes and said, "You know I do not mind being treated a little ugly every once in a while."

YOU-ARE-HERE QUESTION

Is there a place in your life where you justify yourself in speaking "a little ugly?"

The Lord is wanting us to be parents who speak life over our children in order that they would be people who speak it over others. Have you ever noticed a weed or shoot of grass pushing forth from a crack in the concrete? In the same way, we have to look for the fruit of the Spirit, pushing through the cracks in someone else's hard persona. Once we begin to train our eyes to spot godly traits in others, (love, joy, peace, patience, kindness, goodness, faithfulness, gentleness, and self-control), we will be able call forth the fruit.

Part of speaking life is acknowledging growth in others. Here are some ways I'm trying to call forth fruit in my friends and family:

- "I saw you share that toy with your sister. I love your heart for other people."
- "Motherhood can be difficult, but I see the way your eyes shine with love when you look at your children. The Lord is equipping you beautifully for this."
- "I know our God is honored by the decisions you are making."
- "Today you came home and started your homework without me asking. I love that you are growing in responsibility."
- "Your bed was made this morning. You put the biggest smile on my face."
- "I watched you put your phone away when your grandfather walked in the room. That simple gesture shows me your heart that recognizes people are more important than things. I love seeing that in you."
- "You did something today that reminded me of Jesus."

Another significant part of becoming a "life speaker" is being "slow to speak." We have to weigh our thoughts and our words by asking the Lord, "Does this honor You and Your child that I am speaking to?"

In marriage, in parenting, and in friendships, not every thought needs to be spoken aloud. The only One who is equipped to hear and process each thought in your head and each feeling in your heart is our Heavenly Father. He wants you to bring all of yourself to Him. He can help you to sift through your thoughts, categorizing what needs to be left before Him and what can go forth as a blessing from your mouth.

For instance, I love to make people laugh, but sometimes I make the mistake of doing that at someone else's expense. It pains me every time I am confronted in this area. We have to be aware of our humor. Are the stories that you tell about your husband and children ones that bring them honor?

> *The only One who is equipped to hear and process each thought in your head and each feeling in your heart is our Heavenly Father.*

Here is another area where I am learning to shut my mouth. Maybe you are, too. I am learning to let my husband speak. That means letting him finish his story, tell his own joke, explain something to our kids in his own way. Not everything has to be corrected or rushed. This is true with your children as well. Private correction and instruction can be a blessing. The same words spoken in public can feel like a curse.

Psalm 141:3 says, "Set a guard over my mouth. Keep watch over the door of my lips." I am asking the Lord to help me keep my mouth shut when it needs to stay shut.

 ## DROP-A-PIN VERSE

Jesus said, "The first importance is, 'The Lord your God is one, so love the Lord God with all your passion and prayer and intelligence and energy.' And here is the second: Love others as well as you love yourself. There is no other commandment that ranks with these."   Mark 12:29 MSG

DIRECTION QUESTION

Is there someone who could use a reminder of your love? Reach out to them with a word of encouragement.

_____

_____

_____

PRAYER PROMPT

Ask the Lord to help you love Him and think of Him more often. Ask Him to help you see Him in those you love and in those you don't.

_____

_____

_____

DAY 3

When Payton was in early elementary school, we started having some attitude issues with him. The deep sighs, rolling of eyes, and groaning were happening every day. In an effort to stop the trend, Tony and I began to take away his privileges.

His bad attitude continued, so one day Payton and I went to get coffee "to talk." We got our drinks, sat down, and I asked him to tell me what was going on. He told me he was not sure if I wanted to know.

I told him I did.

He said, "The truth is, I am frustrated at you. Every time I am in a deep sleep, you wake me up. Every time I am having fun outside, you call me in. Every time I am enjoying playing games, you tell me I have played enough. Every time I am watching my show, you tell me when my time is up. Every time I want a sweet snack you say, 'You've already had one.' Every time I want to go outside, you remind me to do my homework. Mom, as much as I love you, you are what keeps my life from being perfect."

His list was actually even longer than this; these are just the highlights. I had to smile at his ability to articulate his thoughts. I love every insight that he gives me into his heart, even when it is shocking. From his perspective, I was the only one stopping him. According to him, he was just a mom away from the perfect life.

Years later, the same mom was still between him and something he wanted.

By then, he was in middle school, and I was having the kind of day when my thoughts were running wild. I was reflecting on the many mistakes I have made in parenting. Needless to say, I was not at my most engaging as Payton walked into the room and started talking about his deepest longing for an Xbox.

My mind was somewhere else. On the surface, I was listening but not really interacting. He explained how he was one of the only kids at school who did not have that video game system. In fact, he said, "I actually feel embarrassed sometimes at school because our family does not have an Xbox."

I may have been distracted, but Eden was fully engaged and said, "I think when people are talking to you about their Xboxes, a good thing to say would be, 'Oh yeah? Well I am glad you have an Xbox. But, do you know what I have? An awesome mom. I bet you wish you had an awesome mom.'"

Eden's words brought big smiles to everyone in the room, and they brought me back to the conversation I was missing. No longer was I distracted. Her encouragement breathed life into me. Words have the ability to cut through the clouds and allow the sun to shine.

YOU-ARE-HERE QUESTION

Do you find yourself blaming someone for the challenges in your life?

_____

_____

_____

The Bible tells us that our words bring forth either blessings or curses. We've addressed what it looks like to bless someone with our words, but what does it look like to curse them? It doesn't always come in the form of profanity. Let's ask the Lord to tune our ears to hear where cursing is taking place and we have not realized it. Here are some common ways that people carelessly use their words to curse.

"Well, I would expect that out of that child; he is completely unorganized."

"My husband is always insensitive to my needs."

"My mother-in-law and I could never be friends. She is out to get me."

"My daughter can be rude. She is on the path to becoming a mean girl."

"My son is so negative. He gets that from his father."

"My child's temper is out of control. She comes by it honestly."

You can learn blessing as a second language.

There is hope when we acknowledge that careless words are a battle we all fight. The Lord knows that we require His leading in this area. We learned our native tongue by listening to others speak it. We may have learned a language of cursing by hearing others speak it, as well. If you grew up in a household where cursing was common, know this: You can learn blessing as a second language.

And once you learn it, you will be able to speak it fluently.

DROP-A-PIN VERSE

I call heaven and earth to witness against you that today I have set before you life or death, blessing or curse. Oh, that you would choose life; that you and your children might live! Choose to love the Lord your God and to obey him and to cling to him, for he is your life and the length of your days.

Deuteronomy 30:19-20 TLB

DIRECTION QUESTION

Where do you want to choose life and blessing today?

_____

_____

_____

PRAYER PROMPT

Ask the Lord to make you aware of your words. Ask Him to help you choose life and blessing and to bring quick conviction when you might be unknowingly cursing.

_____

_____

_____

Last year my dad stopped by our house to return something that my mom had borrowed. We had a quick conversation, and then he was out the door. The kids and I watched from the front porch as he climbed in his truck and started pulling away.

Suddenly, he put his truck in park and jumped out in one fluid motion. He ran up to our front porch and hugged me tight. Then he said, "You married an incredible man who loves the Lord. You two are raising four kids who bring smiles to people. You are a mom who I see loving her husband and her kids well. You are doing a great job. I am really proud of you."

My heart nearly burst. I had not realized how hungry I was for that blessing. Tears came immediately. I will treasure that memory for as long as I live on this earth. My dad's words meant a lot to me. His example meant a lot as well. I saw that day the power of slowing down and blessing someone. A few moments can change someone's life.

YOU-ARE-HERE QUESTION

Have you ever received a special encouragement at just the right time?

_____

_____

_____

When we focus on speaking life, we may be tempted to fall into a pattern of flattery. An example of flattery is, "You are the best in the world," or "You are a genius." Your children will begin to see through flattery quickly. Try to bless without exaggeration.

I remember the day one of my boys said, "Please quit saying I am the smartest one in the class. There is actually data out there that proves differently."

> *Take the time to think about how*
> *your words land on someone else's ears.*

It is better to encourage based on facts. Now, I say something like, "I watched you study and prepare for that test. I know you did your best. That makes me proud." That kind of blessing may be toned down, but it is true. And that makes it more effective. Take the time to think about how your words land on someone else's ears.

Remember blessing others will always take time. Be someone who is never in such a hurry that they don't have time to bless.

Sometimes you just have to throw the truck into park, jump out in one fluid motion, and run back to make someone's day.

 ## DROP-A-PIN VERSE

Discover creative ways to encourage others and to motivate them toward acts of compassion, doing beautiful works as expressions of love. This is not the time to pull away and neglect meeting together, as some have formed the habit of doing, because we need each other! In fact, we should come together even more frequently, eager to encourage and urge each other onward as we anticipate that day dawning. Hebrews 10:24-25 TPT

DIRECTION QUESTION

How can you be creative in encouraging others this week?

_____

_____

_____

PRAYER PROMPT

Ask the Lord to deepen your compassion for others. Ask Him to make you aware of people in your life who need a sincere word of encouragement.

_____

_____

_____

When I was 24 years old, Big Brothers Big Sisters hired me to be a recruiter/fundraiser in the Fort Worth area. At that time, the chairman of the board for BBBS was Tom Slone. While we worked together raising money and recruiting people to meet the needs of BBBS, he came along and mentored me.

It strikes me now how unusual that was and still is: a powerful businessman working shoulder to shoulder with a young professional and giving her his time, his advice, and his wisdom. He wanted to see me be successful. He believed in me. He taught me how to channel passion into purpose. He taught me how to close a deal. He taught me how to speak with authority and laugh at my mistakes. The first time I presented to a crowd of nearly 1000, he was there, and I saw him nodding and smiling. He always acknowledged my work. He let me know I mattered.

I was not the only one Tom Slone encouraged.

Encouragement lasts long after
a person leaves this earth.

At his funeral, they asked everyone who had received a handwritten note from Tom to raise their hand. In a packed auditorium, with every seat filled and standing room only, almost every hand went up.

I haven't been able to stop thinking about that sea of raised hands.

Those notes served as anchors holding each of us steady as we moved forward in life. My notes from him connected me to my purpose and to him, a man who took the time to say, "You've got this."

Encouragement lasts long after a person leaves this earth. Jesus knew this and so did Tom. May God bless his family and all those who loved him so much.

YOU-ARE-HERE QUESTION

When was the last time you stopped and wrote a note to encourage someone?

_____

_____

_____

A couple of months back I was really struggling. There were (and still are) some things beyond our control that brought a great deal of stress to our life. I was suffocating under the weight of it all. I needed someone to speak life into me.

Eventually, I made an appointment with a counselor in order to hear myself process some things out loud. It was eye opening for me and so good to get some outside perspective. One of the things that she did was read the words to the classic hymn, "It Is Well with My Soul." It blessed me so much.

When she got to the end, she said, "Right now your 'even so' is off. Things are not well with your soul. Circumstances are rocking you and your emotions. Our goal is to get you back to a place where—even when the difficult things of life occur—you can say once more, 'Even so, it is well with my soul.' I want you to notice the life in her words. She acknowledged my heartache and pointed me to hope.

You and I are on the same journey Paul was on when he talked about having to learn contentment in any and every circumstance. It does not come naturally.

Tony's and my prayers are that the Lord would hear our cry and change the circumstances that bring us grief. But we are feeling more and more content, resting with the attitude of Shadrach, Meshach, and Abednego in Daniel 3:16-18. They knew God could change things, but even if He didn't, they would continue to worship Him. It was well with their souls.

With every day that passes, I am feeling this more and more. I think I am getting my "even so" back on track.

 ## DROP-A-PIN VERSE

Don't be afraid, I've redeemed you. I've called your name. You're mine. When you're in over your head, I'll be there with you. When you're in rough waters, you will not go down. When you're between a rock and a hard place, it won't be a dead end—Because I am God. Isaiah 43:1-3 MSG

DIRECTION QUESTION

Where are you needing to get your "even so" back on track?

_____

_____

_____

PRAYER PROMPT

Ask the Lord to assure your heart that He is with you regardless of circumstance. Ask Him to bring people into your day who will speak life over you.

_____

_____

_____

WHEN YOU NEED ENCOURAGEMENT

When I was a sophomore in high school, I was goofing off with my cousins at my grandparents farm. Their pond had frozen over, and the ice was uncharacteristically thick for a Texas winter. We had spent the morning sliding an old desk chair back and forth to each other across the ice.

At one point, the chair stopped about eight feet from the bank. We had been walking around the edge all morning so I thought I would creep out a little bit further and grab the chair. As I did so, there was a loud cracking sound, and I fell through the ice. Immediately, all my air was gone. My brain knew what to do, but without oxygen, my arms and legs would not work. I'll never forget locking eyes with my cousin and trying to scream. He heard the sound I didn't make and stretched over the ice to pull me out. He saved my life.

In 2017 I fell through the ice spiritually. I was teaching and speaking more than ever, but I was struggling in my spirit. My mind was warring against me, and I had the constant feeling of being overwhelmed. One day, after I sat down from teaching my weekly class at church, my friend Sue came over and said, "Tell me what's going on. I can see it in your eyes."

Sue saw the same thing my cousin had seen years before. I was sinking fast.

From that moment on, she mentored me. She discipled me. She asked hard questions. She helped me dig around in my past and figure out where so much of my doubt had come from. She let me cry. She helped me listen to the Lord. She made sure I was in the Word. She prayed for me and my family constantly. She affirmed who I was. She went the extra mile for me again and again. She helped me grow strong, all in the name of Jesus.

Sue is with Jesus now after a valiant battle with cancer. At her funeral, friend after friend told stories just like mine. Sue knew how to put the courage of Christ in another person's heart, and she spent her life doing so.

I'll forever be thankful that in a room full of people watching me, Sue actually saw what was in my eyes.

I credit both my cousin *and* her for saving my life.

YOU-ARE-HERE QUESTION

Is there a place in motherhood where you feel as if you are sinking?

_____

_____

_____

If you research "What to do when a snake bites" you will learn that if you are bitten by a venomous snake, the faster you can get somewhere to receive anti-venom, the better your chances for a full recovery. If the venom works its way through your body, the results can be disastrous.

Motherhood is much the same. When discouragement strikes, it is best to remember to get help. Sue was able to minister to me in my time of need.

But I also remember others who had asked about my well-being, only to have me reply, "Everything is just fine." I was desperate for encouragement but too proud and too tired to ask for it. If I could go back and talk to myself I would say, *Notice the people trying to reach out for you. They can help.*

Having a child is wonderfully fulfilling, but it is also draining. Prior to becoming a mother, I had never noticed that the world viewed someone holding a baby as an open invitation to give advice. As long as I had a baby in my arms, complete strangers felt at ease offering their unsolicited thoughts. Sometimes the advice blessed and encouraged me. There were other times I found myself standing in the middle of the grocery store, feeling wounded by an interaction I'd just had with a stranger.

The Lord did not give us a "how to" parenting manual. But He did give us what we needed to do this job to His glory: He gave us His Spirit, His Word, and each other.

Think of encouragement as a way to put courage into another person. Encouragement is the anti-venom to bites of this world. It can be found in Scripture. It can be found in prayer. It can be found when people remind you of who you are and who you can be. It can be found in remembering the Lord is partnering with you in this process.

Grab His hand in prayer, and then grab the hand of a sister you see walking the same path you are.

We were never intended to do this alone.

 ## DROP-A-PIN VERSE

So let's do it—full of belief, confident that we are presentable inside and out. Let's keep a firm grip on the promises that keep us going. He always keeps His word. Let's see how inventive we can be in encouraging love and helping out, not avoiding worship together as some do but spurring each other on, especially as we see the day approaching. Hebrews 10:24-25 MSG

DIRECTION QUESTION

Is there someone you feel comfortable asking for encouragement?

_____

_____

_____

PRAYER PROMPT

Ask the Lord to bring people into your life who can put courage in your heart. Ask Him to give you eyes to see those who might be sinking.

_____

_____

_____

During my first pregnancy, I dreamt about my life as a mother. In my imagination, our house was always clean, my baby was always calm, my husband and I always looked happy, and I always looked put together. Being a mom was a lifelong desire, and every piece of it was going to be wonderful. At least, that's what I thought. It did not take long to realize my reality was not going to meet my expectations.

I struggled right out of the gate. I could not believe how tired I was. My mind felt cloudy. Nursing felt awkward. My body hurt. I was overwhelmed with love for our baby, but I was overwhelmed by everything else as well. I remember looking at my husband one night and saying, "I love Payton with my whole heart, but I think we might have ruined our lives."

I said this in complete sincerity. The voice in my mind was questioning my every move. I needed encouragement. Life as a parent was going to require a lot from me, and I wasn't confident that I was ready for it.

Tony reminded me that while motherhood had changed my life, it had not changed the character of God. He was still with me. It was such a simple truth, but I needed to hear it spoken directly to me.

YOU-ARE-HERE QUESTION

What part of motherhood has caught you off guard?

_____

_____

_____

In the Old Testament book of Joshua, the Israelites finally enter the land the Lord intends to be theirs. They are filled with hope for all that this new place will mean for them and their families.

Then they get there. Life doesn't exactly look like what they imagined. The Lord asks them to fight some battles. He requires something of them, and suddenly the Israelites aren't so sure that this is the land they wanted.

In the same way, parenting is full of highs and lows. Our children have brought us our greatest joys. They have also brought us our biggest challenges. We can be in the center of God's will, and things may still feel difficult. Joseph and Mary were doing exactly what the Lord would have them to do; they were exactly where they were supposed to be, and the son of God was still born in a barn. That certainly wasn't what Mary expected. Life may look different than what you expected, but here is the truth you can cling to: The Lord is with you wherever you go.

> We can be in the center of God's will,
> and things may still feel difficult.

Our God does the best on-the-job training. As you develop in your skill, you will slip every now and then. If you have made mistakes as a mother, you are in great company. We all have. Parenting provides the opportunity to grow as you lead your treasure of a child towards the Lord. It is not without hardship. It is not without momentary failure. It is not without discouraging seasons, but the Almighty God is behind you, beside you, and even now, He is going before you. Let's work together to make crying out to the Lord our first response. He is the ultimate Help, able in any and every situation to do more than we can ask or imagine. Find a friend you can pray with.

In addition to leaning on Him, let's lean on each other. We were not meant to do this on our own. The Lord created you to need others. When He creates a need, He also intends to meet that need as well. So commit to a community that encourages you to be who the Lord is calling you to be. Connect with a mentor who knows you. Find someone who has been where you want to go. Seek them out. Let them join the Lord in giving you courage and hope for the journey ahead.

 DROP-A-PIN VERSE

Be strong and courageous. Do not be afraid; do not be discouraged for the Lord your God will be with you wherever you go.

Joshua 1:9

DIRECTION QUESTION

What task in your life feels easier or at least more doable when you remember the Lord is with you?

_____

_____

_____

PRAYER PROMPT

Ask the Lord to give you a fresh view of your obstacles and make you strong and courageous in Jesus name.

_____

_____

_____

One morning when Shelby was a toddler, she was particularly grumpy. As I was holding her, I said, "Let's try to list off everyone who loves you."

As she and I alternated calling out names, her little face grew brighter and brighter. It was a mind-changing and mood-altering experience. It shifted the course of our day. Grumbling-turned-to-laughing is one of my favorite miracles of God.

> *Grumbling-turned-to-laughing is one of my favorite miracles of God.*

He can work the same miracle in a mother that He can work in a child. Sometimes, I need to slow down, listen, and remember. Scripture tells us the Lord is watching over us. I think often of 2 Chronicles 16:9: "The eyes of the Lord search the whole earth in order to strengthen those whose hearts are fully committed to Him."

I like to think of His eyes stopping on me, on my family, and on my friends.

YOU-ARE-HERE QUESTION

What is your most consistent repeating thought regarding yourself? Does it line up with the fact that you are loved?

_____

_____

_____

Motherhood can be lonely at times. We can move so quickly that we forget we have purpose and are surrounded by love. On days when I am feeling the ache of a life lived too fast, I ask the Lord for His eyes to stop on me for a bit. When I am needing encouragement sometimes the best thing I can do for my soul is ask the Lord to fill it.

Every great movie has a soundtrack. What is the soundtrack to your life? Make no mistake, if you do not choose one, the enemy will choose it for you. What song does your heart play in tough moments? Think of it as your soul soundtrack.

For years, the go-to praise song on my soul soundtrack was "Starry Night" by Chris August. Something about hearing the words "I'm giving my life to the only One who makes the moon reflect the sun," brought me comfort and hope.

Think about teaching your children to create a soul soundtrack for themselves. They need a song inside to combat the enemy as much as you do. Help them choose a go-to praise song that can encourage their hearts when they are down. The Lord created our hearts to sing so let's do it.

 ## DROP-A-PIN VERSE

Your God is present among you, a strong warrior to save you. Happy to have you back, He'll calm you with His love and delight you with His songs. Zephaniah 3:17

DIRECTION QUESTION

What song is on your soul soundtrack?

_____

_____

_____

PRAYER PROMPT

Ask the Lord to remind you of His love. Ask Him to remind you of your reasons to sing.

_____

_____

_____

A few years back, I was going through a drive-thru with my son Payton. As I got my order, I took a quick sip and realized they had put some type of syrup in my coffee that I had not ordered. I said nicely, "There's something in this drink that I didn't order."

The barista was gracious and said she would make me a new drink immediately. Even this minor confrontation made Payton uncomfortable, and he told me so. He ended his speech with a line that has stuck with me, "Do you ever mention it to them when they make your drink right?"

The facts are, if my drink had been made correctly, I would not have even interacted with that barista. I have a tendency to make a comment only if something went wrong. That day I decided to change. I wanted to notice when things went right.

So when the barista made my drink the next time we were in the drive-thru, I took a sip and exclaimed, "Wow. This is great. Thanks." or "I needed this. Thank you for making it for me." In an effort to be intentional with my appreciation, I think I went overboard a few times.

One day as I sat in the drive-thru, I realized I had left my wallet at home. I pulled up to the window and said, "I'm sorry. I have no money, and I don't even have enough change in my car console to pay for that cup of coffee."

The barista smiled and said, "Don't worry about it; this one's on us."

Taken aback I said, "But I don't have time to come back later and pay."

She smiled again and said, "Just take it."

The barista beside her leaned over and echoed her statement, "We really want you to have it."

I laughed and asked, "Why?"

She said, "This coffee makes your day. Out of all of our customers you are the only one who ever comments about how happy it makes you. We all love hearing what you say. It encourages us. So this coffee is on us. We'll take care of you today because we know it makes you happy."

I thanked them, smiled, and then pondered their words all the way home. That drive-thru line wraps around the building on most days, and I usually go once a week. Yet my goofy encouragement over a latte was enough to make me stand out in hundreds of cars.

Are you looking to make a difference in this world? May I suggest you encourage someone? May I suggest you notice what they are doing right?

Your ability to encourage can change someone's day, life, and even the impact they have on this world.

YOU-ARE-HERE QUESTION

When was the last time you spoke up when you noticed someone doing something right?

_____

_____

_____

Do not let anything keep you from being an encourager. We live in a society that only speaks up when things are wrong. Begin today to notice the good that is all around you. This is the heart of Jesus, who saw the good all around Him and called it out in others.

Encourage someone by speaking words of blessing over their life. And on the days when you feel you are accomplishing nothing of value, sit down and write someone you know a letter of encouragement. No one has ever opened a handwritten encouragement note and thought, "I could have done without this today."

> *No one has ever opened a handwritten encouragement note and thought, "I could have done without this today."*

Do you want to do something lasting? Encourage! Your words will echo for eternity in someone's heart and mind.

 ## DROP-A-PIN VERSE

And let us consider how to stir up one another to love and good works, not neglecting to meet together, as is the habit of some, but encouraging one another, and all the more as you see the Day drawing near.   Hebrews 10:24-25 ESV

DIRECTION QUESTION

Who can you encourage in your family this week? How?

_____

_____

_____

PRAYER PROMPT

Ask the Lord to help you notice people doing right. Ask Him to open your eyes to see family, friends, and strangers who are blessing you through their daily presence in your life.

_____

_____

_____

DAY 5

In 2009, Tony's dad died unexpectedly. We were crushed. I remember posting about it on Facebook before we left to go meet with the funeral home. By the time we came back from that meeting, we had many comments from friends who were letting us know they were hurting with us. People posted prayers, scriptures, and encouragement.

We were greatly acknowledged online, and those gestures carried us through those first difficult days, but soon we felt alone. Our grief was deep, and we did a lot of living in survival mode. Somehow the online comments that had once meant so much felt hollow and empty. I needed a person to show up in the flesh and love us.

On a day when we were feeling particularly low, a friend showed up unannounced with a meal for our family. I remember thinking it was the best meal I had ever eaten. Years later, I don't remember what we ate, but I do remember the refreshment that filled our home when that friend walked in. She gave us food for our bodies, but her presence felt like oxygen for our souls.

That memory is a constant reminder to me to reach out in person. In a world swimming with likes, hearts, and comments from acquaintances, we have to admit this isn't the way we were created to connect. Social media can become a counterfeit of true community.

YOU-ARE-HERE QUESTION

To whom can you make a face-to-face gesture of encouragement?

Social media can sometimes look like a good substitute for face-to-face time with a friend. But in truth, it's not. It is a great snack that can sustain you for a time. But, you cannot live on snacks. You need real nourishment. So concentrate on making time to meet in person.

Sure, there will be times when reaching out through social media is the appropriate response, but we do well to ask ourselves, "Is this the best I can do?" The answer may be yes, but the answer also may be no. Do not assume you know which one it is. When you least expect it, the Holy Spirit may nudge your heart to go to the funeral, make the hospital visit, drop off the meal, or write the note with a real pen and real paper. These kinds of meaningful gestures are twice as valuable as they used to be because they are rare. And they are not accomplished by people who have an empty schedule and "nothing better to do." Almost no one has an empty schedule anymore. The only way a meaningful gesture will be accomplished these days is if someone makes the effort to rearrange and reprioritize.

There are certain days that I know social media is going to be hard on my heart. Do you have those? Do you have days where you can tell your soul is searching for something deeper than what you will find on a social media platform? On days like that I try to concentrate on encouraging. I say out loud, "Lord, if I get on Facebook (or Instagram or Twitter, etc...) I am committing to encourage at least three people before I do anything else." My mind sees things differently if I am looking through the filter of encouragement rather than comparison.

The lesson is simple: May social media be the last place we turn when we need to receive and the first place we turn when we want to give.

DROP-A-PIN VERSE

A man of many companions may come to ruin, but there is a friend who sticks closer than a brother. Proverbs 18:24 ESV

DIRECTION QUESTION

How can you use your time on social media to put courage into the hearts of your friends?

_____

_____

_____

PRAYER PROMPT

Ask the Lord to give you new eyes as you scroll. Ask Him to help you see those who need your face-to-face encouragement.

_____

_____

_____

WHAT GOD HAS GIVEN YOU IN YOUR MARRIAGE

DAY 1

Years ago when my grandfather was dying, my dad asked him, "If you could live any part of your life over again what would you choose."

My grandfather said, "I loved falling in love with your mom. I'd do that again in a heartbeat."

Twenty years in, and I would echo his words. I loved falling in love with Tony, and I love being in love with Tony.

Every once in a while, during a day when kids are crying, teens are needing to be driven to the next event, everyone is hungry, and someone remembers a project that is due tomorrow, Tony and I will look at each other, and one of us will say, "This is the life we always dreamed of, isn't it?"

Then we both laugh out loud because we know we never dreamed of this. But here's the truth: While not many dream of living through those particular situations, many people do long for the camaraderie that those experiences produce. Trying times submitted to the Lord produce good things in our lives.

Jesus works in the highs and lows
in equal measure.

Our life together has had highs and lows, but Tony's steadiness has anchored us through them all. He is a man of few words married to a woman who never runs out of them. He is a man of organization and plans married to a spontaneous woman with a *That-pile-isn't-bothering-anyone* mentality. On some days all our quirks together make for a lot of fun. On other days, they combine to cause hurt feelings and arguments.

Jesus works in the highs and lows in equal measure. Conflict does not throw Him off. Humans grow concerned in times of heartache. We begin to doubt ourselves and our marriage. Jesus reminds us that even in the middle of mayhem we can be of good cheer, for He has overcome the world. In marriage we look to our overcoming Savior, to Jesus. He is the One who has always been with us. We will hold onto Him and to each other until we see eternity.

YOU-ARE-HERE QUESTION

How are you holding onto Jesus in your marriage?

_____

_____

_____

Even though marriage might look different than what we imagined, it is producing in us the fruits of the Spirit. We are in the process of becoming the people the Lord intended. He redeems everything. He is Lord over every hard situation, every hurt feeling, every "I wish this had never happened," and He is at work. So, on the days my prayers consist of frustration and confusion, I remember the God we serve and His ability to turn defeat into victory.

We see this so vividly at the cross of Jesus. The Son of God takes His last breath and dies. His disciples are left deep in grief and feeling as if they have misunderstood everything. They lose sight of Jesus and what He promised. Yet in three days, Jesus is resurrected and enters His victorious inheritance.

The life you dreamed of is often born out of moments you wanted to avoid. We can't have the victory of Christ without first experiencing his death. So don't lose sight of Jesus in your marriage. The same power that raised Him from the dead is at work in your home and in your family

DROP-A-PIN VERSE

Put your hope in the Lord, for with the Lord is unfailing love and with him is full redemption. Psalm 130:7

DIRECTION QUESTION

Where are you currently needing the Lord to bring His resurrection power?

_____

_____

_____

PRAYER PROMPT

Ask God to keep reminding you that He is a redeeming God. Ask that His power would be displayed in your marriage.

_____

_____

_____

DAY 2

One of my love languages is words of affirmation so when I found a note pad with a love note template printed on every page, I knew I needed it. I didn't want it so I could write love notes to Tony, but so he could write love notes to me. On the top of the page, it read, *LOVE NOTE*. Then it had boxes for *TO* and *FROM*. Finally, there was a box for writing that began with a prompt: *I love you because ...*

I mean, all he had to do was fill out a couple of boxes and complete a sentence. I gave it to Tony and said, "I will be beside myself if you use this."

And I am. Every. Single. Time.

Whoever made the statement, "If I have to ask you for it, it doesn't count," was not telling the truth. It counts.

I want to love Tony better. Sometimes I instinctively know how to do that, but other times he has to let me know what that looks like. It's a gift we give each other. I spent the first few years of our marriage disappointed that Tony could not read my mind. He spent time frustrated that I couldn't anticipate his needs. Then we realized we got married because we were committed to helping each other in all things. I can help him know me better, and he can help me know him better. I love flowers, and he loves when the clean laundry doesn't live on our kitchen table. We are both working on loving each other in the ways the other one enjoys. We give each other insight into each other and into Jesus. May He continue to lead us on.

When was the last time you asked your spouse, "How can I love you better?" (Do it today!)

_____

_____

_____

Before I got married, a group of people that I worked with hosted a "wedding advice" shower for me. My boss gave me some advice that has stuck with me through the years, "Right now, you and Tony are walking through a lush land. Everything is green and full of life, but at some point, you two will walk into the desert. Hold tightly to the things that you love. You will need those to sustain you in the desert."

His advice meant a lot to me then, but it means even more now. I appreciated the fact that he acknowledged that even the best marriages have challenges. Because they do. But here's what I know: There is difficulty, but there is also incredible joy when two people who are committed to each other and to the Lord live their lives side by side.

You cannot fight a battle you never acknowledge.

The enemy knows that good, happy, and thriving marriages provide a strong foundation for children. He wants to destroy your marriage to hurt you, yes, but also to get a foothold in the lives of your children. Recognizing that the enemy wants to sow seeds of discouragement and doubt into your marriage helps you see more clearly when your marriage is under attack.

You cannot fight a battle you never acknowledge. Watch for anger, bitterness, and aggravation. Watch the conversation you have in your head about your spouse. Commit that you will not hold any of these things in a way that the enemy could use.

Side note: I am well aware that this book will be read by many who are single parents or have felt the pain of divorce. Do not let the enemy weigh you down with discouragement. Press on. There is no victory Jesus cannot win on your behalf or on behalf of your child. He is able to double your impact if you are parenting alone. And if you are parenting with a husband or ex-husband who does not have a relationship with Jesus or does not participate in healthy parenting, God can double your impact in that situation, as well. Cling to God and trust that He can be the Father you wish your kids had.

 DROP-A-PIN VERSE

Watch what God does, and then you do it, like children who learn proper behavior from their parents. Mostly what God does is love you. Keep company with Him and learn a life of love. Observe how Christ loved us. His love was not cautious but extravagant. He didn't love in order to get something from us but to give everything of himself to us. Love like that. Ephesians 5:1-2 MSG

DIRECTION QUESTION

Where can you give your husband a small indicator of your support and care in *his* love language?

_____

_____

_____

PRAYER PROMPT

Ask the Lord to help you rely on His unfailing love. Ask Him to help you love like He does, not cautiously but extravagantly.

_____

_____

_____

When Payton and Benjamin were toddlers, leaving the house was difficult. They were unpredictable, and it always felt like we were walking around with a time bomb. Was someone going to get hungry and start to cry? Was someone going to miss their nap? What if one of them had a dirty diaper? So many things caused me stress. I thought life would be much easier if we just stayed home.

There was only one problem. Tony has always been one who wants to spend his weekends on the go.

No problem. I blessed him to go and spend his Saturday however he wanted. I told him the boys and I would just enjoy our routine at home. Then one day Tony said he was unhappy with this arrangement. He had worked all week, and he wanted to spend his Saturdays with us. He missed us during the week and didn't want to be away from us on the weekends as well. Even if it was something as simple as running errands, he preferred that we would go with him.

I remember looking at him and saying, "It's just easier if the boys and I stay home."

His reply has stuck with me through the years. He said, "We didn't sign up for *easy*; we signed up for *together*."

From that point on, we all ran around together on Saturdays. Some days the boys had meltdowns, and sometimes they missed their naps. While those things mattered on the days they happened, in the long term, the details had no lasting impact. The one thing that has had a lasting impact was our togetherness. It wasn't always easy, but in the end it was worth it.

Is there a place where you have chosen *easy* over *together*?

_____

_____

_____

I love asking people about the first trait that drew them to their spouse. It's always fun to hear what caused people to fall in love. Sometimes, I will follow-up by asking, "Do you *still* love that trait?"

Usually women will laugh and acknowledge how much has changed since that time. I want to encourage you: The qualities that drew you to your husband are still there. They might look different, but they are still there. Every area of your life has changed since you and your man fell in love.

> *Growth and change are positive, but*
> *the enemy wants to cast them as negative.*

The enemy wants to discourage you and say, "He is not who he was."

The truth is, he is not. But neither are you. You are both growing and changing. The Lord wants to work though this growth and change to bring you both closer to Him. Growth and change are positive, but the enemy wants to cast them as negative.

For years, I thought the best way to bring about change in Tony was to tell him what he needed to work on. It took some time for me to realize that my words were not effective. My speeches and lectures actually were roadblocks to the change the Lord was trying to bring about. The only One who can bring about change or movement in our spouse, or in each of us, is our God. There is one Holy Spirit, and I am not Him.

As eager as I was to work on Tony, the Lord was just as eager to work on me.

Side Note: I am writing about some ways to strengthen our marriages, but I want to acknowledge that I am not a counselor. In some ways, the messages in this book can be considered "preventative care." I hope it is a blessing to everyone reading. However, I know that some of you may be struggling mightily in your marriages. I want to encourage you to seek professional help if you sense that it is needed. When it comes to your physical body, if you find a lump, you do not call your doctor and schedule an appointment for six months later. You call your doctor and try to get in as soon as possible. So please, if you have an issue that requires immediate attention in your marriage, do not treat it as something that can wait. Find a mentor, call a minister, or talk to a counselor. Whatever you do, do not turn this page without a plan.

 ## DROP-A-PIN VERSE

So, chosen by God for this new life of love, dress in the wardrobe God picked out for you: compassion, kindness, humility, quiet strength, discipline. Be even-tempered, content with second place, quick to forgive an offense. Forgive as quickly and completely as the Master forgave you. And regardless of what else you put on, wear love. It's your basic, all-purpose garment. Never be without it.
                                        Colossians 3:14-17 MSG

DIRECTION QUESTION

Is there a place in your marriage where you have been trying to take the Holy Spirit's job?

_____

_____

_____

PRAYER PROMPT

Ask the Lord to help you trust that He is doing a mighty work in your husband. Ask Him to help you make sure to always wear love.

_____

_____

_____

I like my music turned up loud. One day it was so loud, I didn't realize I had hit a mailbox with the back of my car until it dragged down the side and past my passenger window.

Good news: That mailbox was sturdy, so we don't need to replace it.

Even better news: I married Tony, who always prays that the Lord will give him opportunities to show the love and grace of Jesus.

Here I am, Lord, send me.

If Tony had a dollar for every time I have backed into a mailbox, a dumpster, his truck, or our house, he would be able to buy himself a really nice dinner. He is a constant source of grace in my life. It's not that he doesn't get frustrated. It's not that he doesn't need a few minutes to breathe deeply. It is just that he doesn't hold onto it.

When people ask me about the key to a successful marriage, I usually say grace. Tony and I can fight like champions, and through the years we have said things we wish we had not said. But we love the Lord and each other. We always come back to grace.

YOU-ARE-HERE QUESTION

Where are you in need of grace? Where are you needing to extend it?

_____

_____

_____

Marriage provides an incredible opportunity to work toward unity on a daily basis. Tony and I disagree about some things, but we agree that the Lord is in control. We trust God to move us closer to each other as we move closer to Him.

One of the ways He moves us toward unity is through prayer. Each marriage is going to look different in this area. Do you pray together at meals? With your children? Before big decisions? Whether your answer is, "The last time we prayed together was our wedding," "We have never prayed together," or "We pray together daily," start asking God to move in your prayer life as a couple. Let's acknowledge that the first step to praying with your husband is praying yourself.

> *Don't let anything or anyone rob you of meaningful time with the most important person in your life.*

Another thing you can do to encourage unity in your marriage is putting your kids to bed! You and your husband need time together alone, and your children need sleep. If you can coordinate those two things, you are in for daily joy. Let your husband know that your end goal is that you two would have more time together. Remember your children will be either a blessing that draws you and your husband together or a blessing that the enemy uses to wedge you apart.

It is not enough just to spend time together. Make sure your time together is used well.

- Dock that phone.
- Turn off that TV.
- Call your friend tomorrow.

Don't let anything or anyone rob you of meaningful time with the most important person in your life.

 DROP-A-PIN VERSE

If you have gotten anything at all out of following Christ, if His love has made any difference in your life, if being in a community of the Spirit means anything to you, if you have a heart, if you care- then do me a favor: Agree with each other, love each other, be deep-spirited friends. Don't push your way to the front; don't sweet-talk your way to the top. Put yourself aside, and help others get ahead. Don't be obsessed with getting your own advantage. Forget yourself long enough to lend a helping hand.

Philippians 2:1-4 MSG

DIRECTION QUESTION

Where do you need to forget yourself long enough to lend a helping hand?

_____

_____

_____

PRAYER PROMPT

Ask the Lord to give you and your husband a desire to pray together. Ask Him to help you get your kids to bed at a decent hour and make them deep sleepers. Ask Him to make you aware of things that are robbing your time together.

_____

_____

_____

DAY 5

Our honeymoon wasn't a fairy tale. There were many great moments, but also some stressful ones. We missed our flight. We had our first major argument. (I had always thought Tony was wonderful but that was before he disagreed with me.) I lost my purse. The airline lost my luggage. (Regardless of what anyone says, I was actually someone who did want to have clothes on my honeymoon.)

I have a vivid memory of being in the shower and thinking, *I don't even know this man* ... and stepping out of the shower to lock the door. We laugh about that now.

You should know that in our last session of premarital counseling, our counselor had asked if there were any significant topics that had not been discussed. He wanted us to examine every area that we anticipated strain in marriage. Tony thought for a moment and said he had something to share.

I waited to hear some big bomb drop.

His "big bomb" was he did not like vomit, and he wasn't sure how he would handle it when I got sick. I remember assuring Tony that it would be a long time before he found out how he'd handle it because I had not thrown up in years.

Well.

Of course I got sick right away, and threw up throughout our last night in our honeymoon suite.

A wedding may change a relationship status, but a husband and wife remain two people who desperately needed Jesus.

On our honeymoon we had fun and laughed a lot, but we also got an introduction to life. Being in love did not mean our humanness disappeared.

A wedding may change a relationship status, but a husband and wife remain two people who desperately needed Jesus.

YOU-ARE-HERE QUESTION

Where is your humanness evident in your marriage?

_____

_____

_____

What are some ways two people who desperately need Jesus can cultivate love in their marriage?

We look to the Lord to secure.
You recognize that you get your value and affirmation from Jesus. It is only in Him you are complete. You ask our God to be the One on whom your self-esteem rests. You trust the Lord with your heart.

We look to the Lord to sustain.
Trust the Lord to give you what you need on a day-to-day basis. Do more than just survive your marriage. Ask the Lord to make your marriage a life-giving blessing for everyone involved.

We look to the Lord to forgive.
Do not hold past mistakes over your spouse. Ask the Lord to give you a heart that desires to go the second mile (Matthew 5:41).

We look to the Lord to focus.
Make a list of ten reasons why you love being married to your

husband and post this list for both of you to see. Train your eyes to look for his strengths and learn to focus on what the Lord is focusing on. One of the enemy's favorite tricks is to get us to focus on our spouse's flaws while completely ignoring our own.

We recognize the importance of sex.
Enjoy your sex life. Our culture says that marriage is where sex goes to die. What an incredible lie from Satan. The Bible does not just allow for sex, the Bible celebrates it. (Read Song of Solomon!) The Lord is interested in your sex life. Ask Him to bless it.

 DROP-A-PIN VERSE

> *Do not be misled: No one makes a fool of God. What a person plants, he will harvest. The person who plants selfishness, ignoring the needs of others—ignoring God!—harvests a crop of weeds. All they will have to show for their life is weeds. But the one who plants in response to God, letting God's Spirit do the growth work in them, harvests a crop of real life, eternal life. So let's not allow ourselves to get fatigued doing good. At the right time, we will harvest a good crop if we do not give up, or quit. Right now, therefore, every time we get the chance, let us work for the benefit of all, starting with the people closest to us.* Galatians 6:7-10 MSG

DIRECTION QUESTION

What point are you going to work on in your marriage this week?

_____

_____

_____

PRAYER PROMPT

Ask the Lord to make you aware of the seeds you are planting in your marriage. Ask Him to keep you from getting fatigued in doing good.

_____

_____

_____

HOW PRAYER CHANGES YOU

I'll never forget when Payton started his first season of tackle football. He was excited. I was terrified. Not wanting to cause him concern, I did my best to conceal my fears and rarely spoke of them out loud. In the early morning hours before I woke Payton for his practice, I would spend time on my knees. I did my best to surrender those negative emotions. Then, as I drove Payton to school, he and I would pray together again. I was in constant conversation with the Lord, and I felt good about that.

Imagine my surprise at the conversation overheard after the first football game:

Tony: "What did you think about your game?"
Payton: "It was terrible. I missed a lot of tackles. I am frustrated with myself. Mom prays for me every morning on the way to school. I know she means well, but she is freaking me out. The things she prays stay with me."

Tony noticed that I was listening in, probably because I was waving my arms and jumping, pointing at Payton behind his back and mouthing, "What in the world? This is not my fault!"

Tony waved me off. I could hardly wait for Payton to go to bed so Tony and I could talk.

When that moment came, Tony asked me to tell him what I had been praying with Payton.

I responded with confidence, "Freedom from concussion, strong neck, knees, arms, wrists ..."

Through prayer the Savior of the World
signs His name with mine.

As I went over my laundry list of body parts, Tony understood the problem. He said, "We do want protection of every one of those things for him. Every single one of them. Remember though, when you are praying, you come to prayer from a position of strength, not from a position of fear."

Pray from a position of strength. Those words continue to ripple through my life. It is an exhilarating thought: Through prayer the Savior of the world signs His name with mine.

YOU-ARE-HERE QUESTION

Has there been a time you have let fear direct your prayers?

_____

_____

_____

No mother wants to imagine her child—or any child, for that matter—on a battlefield. Yet that is the world into which we were all born. In order to survive, we have to remember that we are connected to power through our victorious Jesus.

The enemy comes in and wants to take our solid position of faith and replace it with the quicksand of fear. Don't let him. Pray for strength to match the battle we face. Pray for clear vision that we would see the true enemy. Don't let fear lead your words. Take your position and offer your prayer. You pray from strength.

I am talking to myself a lot more lately. My kids, ever watching, have noticed and asked, "Mom, are you talking to yourself or to God?"

Truthfully, it's a little of both. The heartache in this world is escalating. We all can feel it. But I can't let that heartache drown out my voice. I'll admit, sometimes it's shaky, but it's still there.

So if you listen close, you might just hear me whispering, *Victory is sure. He has overcome the world.* I'm trusting that my whisper of faith, covered in the blood of a risen Savior, becomes a shout that echoes in the spiritual realm.

 DROP-A-PIN VERSE

Be prepared. You're up against far more than you can handle on your own. Take all the help you can get, every weapon God has issued, so that when it's all over but the shouting you'll still be on your feet. Truth, righteousness, peace, faith, and salvation are more than words. Learn how to apply them. You'll need them throughout your life. God's word is an indispensable weapon. In the same way, prayer is essential in this ongoing warfare. Pray hard and long. Pray for your brothers and sisters. Keep your eyes open. Keep each other's spirits up so that no one falls behind or drops out. Ephesians 6:17-18 MSG

DIRECTION QUESTION

How can you make prayer part of your daily life?

_____

_____

_____

PRAYER PROMPT

Ask the Lord to anchor you in victory.

_____

_____

_____

As a small child, I loved going to spend the night with my grandparents. On one particular night, I had a hard time sleeping, and I felt fear rising in my heart. Lying there alone with my thoughts, I got more and more terrified. I mustered the courage to run to my grandmother's room to tell her I was scared. She prayed with me and took me back to my bed.

I lay there for a bit and still felt fear gripping my heart. I went back to my grandmother and said, "Your prayer did not work. I still feel scared."

She pulled me onto her lap, held me close, and said, "Let's pray again. The Lord heard us the first time. Now I want *you* to hear us."

She asked the Lord to calm my fears, and then she asked Him to help me believe our prayers made a difference. As she tucked me back into my bed, she said, "Sometimes it helps to say out loud, 'God, I believe You've heard my prayer.'"

I went to bed, and once again the fear rose, but I reminded myself that the Lord had heard my prayer. I said it over and over again. My grandmother taught me about faith that night. I am still learning to listen for His whisper above the noise. It's not a voice that immediately takes away fear, it's a voice that tells me "I'm here with you, right in the middle of this."

While we may not share the same fears, we do share the same enemy. Satan works in panic, chaos, and shortness of breath. Satan rushes. The Lord stills. Satan sends us into a free fall of emotions and thoughts. Our God steadies.

|||||||||||||||||||||||||||||||||||||||||||||||||||||||||||||||||||||||||||||||||||||||||||||||||||||||||||||||||||||

What prayer are you currently praying that you need to close with the words, "God, I believe You've heard my prayer?"

_____

_____

_____

God's plan was that we would live our lives in conversation with Him. There is no right or wrong way to pray. When your child was learning to speak, your intention was not to correct as much as it was to understand. Your priority was to know your child's heart. You were not concerned with proper pronunciations. You were thrilled to hear your child start communicating. It is the same with God. He does not need you to sound a certain way, He wants to hear your heart.

The purpose of prayer is to pour out our hearts before God. If you are a list maker, write out the things that are concerning you. If you are a runner or walker, talk to Him as you would an exercise partner. If you meditate, focus on our God and His power. If you are someone who talks to yourself as you work, invite the Creator of the world into the conversation.

I spend time with the Lord in the morning. For years I trained myself to make God my first thought. I have worked on making that a habit. There are still days when I wake up, and my first thought is, "I forgot to get dog food," but I am getting better at acknowledging the Lord first. I try to listen to worship music to get my heart and my mind centered on God. Then I spend time in the Bible and bring before the Lord the joys and cares of my heart. After that initial time in prayer I am in constant conversation with the Lord throughout the day.

> *Prayer creates an equation only God could solve:*
> *Our weakness + Him = Strength.*

What I just described is what *my* prayer life looks like. My husband's prayer life looks totally different. My four kids each pray in different ways. I want to tell you I spent years trying to reproduce myself in each of my family members. I was arrogant in letting them know I wished their commitment to prayer looked more like mine. Until one day I felt the Lord speak to my heart, "You are praying for growth in your family, but then you are hindering it with your words and actions."

My grandmother did not tell me how to pray the night fear crept into my heart. She just told me to hold onto the truth that God always hears what I offer. I encourage you today, regardless of what it looks like, to offer your prayer.

Prayer creates an equation only God could solve: Our weakness + Him = Strength.

My faith in God has not made me fearless. I can still feel fear. We may feel fear, but we don't build our house on it. Just as the blood of Christ flows over us and through us, so does His strength.

That whispered prayer of faith, "Lord, I believe You've heard my prayer," sounds small here on earth. But it is a roar in the heavens.

Our whisper + God's power = Mountains moved.

 DROP-A-PIN VERSE

Don't worry about anything; instead pray about everything. Tell God what you need, and thank him for all He has done. Then you will experience God's peace, which exceeds anything we can understand. His peace will guard your hearts and minds as you live in Christ. Philippians 4:6-7 NLT

DIRECTION QUESTION

Have you been wrestling with some things that you haven't carried in conversation to the Lord? List them here.

_____

_____

_____

PRAYER PROMPT

Read over your list and imagine yourself transferring ownership of each of these things from you to the Lord. Ask the Lord to remind you that He is in control.

_____

_____

_____

When Payton was a newborn, I went shopping on a day when it seemed everyone in the world had had the same idea. As I was circling the parking lot looking for a space, a truck started to back out. It hit the passenger side of my car with a loud crunch.

Payton and I were fine. My car was not. I pulled over so that the other driver and I could take a look at the damage.

Payton started to cry. The man and I tried to exchange insurance information, but Payton's cries slowed down the process. As I tried to comfort my baby and copy information at the same time, the man, who by this time had lit up a cigarette, said, "It's hot out here. This is taking too long. Why don't you hand me your baby so you can concentrate."

I said, " I am fine."

> *We are never going to be able to give God the things that mean the most to us, if we do not know Him.*

The man insisted, "Just give me the baby, and we'll get this done."

I looked at him and said, "Sir, I do not know you. There is no way I am going to let you hold my baby."

I think about this story often when I am struggling with giving something to the Lord.

We are never going to be able to give God the things that mean the most to us, if we do not know Him.

YOU-ARE-HERE QUESTION

Do you trust the Lord with the things that matter to you?

_____

_____

_____

The call to prayer is a call to trust. Prayer is believing that one of the best ways you can invest your time is speaking to God. It's knowing that these conversations make a difference. Even when we can't see it or feel it, our prayers move us closer to the heart of our Heavenly Father.

It's important that we get specific when we pray. If we aren't specific when we ask the question, we won't notice when the answer comes. Trust the Lord enough to ask specifically.

Ultimately, _He_ is the answer.

 ## DROP-A-PIN VERSE

Trust in Him at all times, O people; pour out your heart before Him; God is a refuge for us. Psalm 62:8

DIRECTION QUESTION

When God becomes your refuge, how does life look different?

_____

_____

_____

PRAYER PROMPT

Ask the Lord to remind you of who He is. Ask Him to bring you peace. Then pause and take deep breaths. Allow Him to calm your heart.

_____

_____

_____

My brother Andy stopped our jeep at the top of a canyon at our parent's ranch and pointed to the other side. He said, "Do you see those deer over there?"

After I looked at where he was pointing, I could squint and see two little four-legged specks on the horizon. "How did you ever spot them?" I asked.

Andy replied, "You have to train your eyes to look for movement. The landscape was still, but one of those deer flicked its ear forward. The movement stood out against the stillness."

I wanted to train my spiritual eyes. So I began to ask God for them. I committed that each day as I buckled in our children, we would talk about looking for the movement of God in our lives. As the Lord was training me to see Him, I wanted to be training my children as well. This eventually evolved into us saying, "How do you see God's glory?"

> *The world is usually rushing along*
> *in the same direction, and that's why the people*
> *of God so often stand out.*

Each day as we ran our errands, drove to preschool, did our everyday things, we began looking for God's glory. And we started noticing it in ways we never had before. When Payton bumped his head and a huge knot formed, we talked about God's glory. The Lord had revealed His power through Payton's body responding in that way. When Benjamin got a stomach virus, we talked about God's glory. The Lord had revealed His power through Benjamin's body knowing when to get the virus out, even when he himself did not know something was in there.

The more we have trained our eyes, the more we are seeing our ever-working God. And as we see Him more, our prayer life grows deeper and deeper. We look for Him in the good and the hard.

You can train your eyes to notice the movement of the Lord, too. The world is usually rushing along in the same direction, and that's why the people of God so often stand out. We aren't supposed to look like the world. If we do, it's time to ask ourselves why. When the Lord says, "Be still and know that I am God," He is wanting the movement of the world to be noticeable.

YOU-ARE-HERE QUESTION

How are you being still and noticing the Lord?

_____

_____

_____

If you are someone who has grown up in the church, you will often hear people refer to "quiet time." In the Bible, we see Jesus withdrawing to pray often. We don't know how long Jesus spent, praying alone. We just know that time with His Father was a priority.

I know mothers who can feel immense guilt if they are not reading at least a chapter a day or spending at least thirty minutes in quiet time. The point is not the amount of reading or the amount of time. The point is connecting to your Father. I love the days I wake up earlier than my children and have time for uninterrupted prayer. But that does not always happen.

Do not let the enemy tell you, "You should wait until it's quiet. You should wait until you have more time. You should wait until you can focus." You can abide in Christ anywhere, any time.

Motherhood is one of the toughest balancing acts around. It's knowing when to hold tightly and when to let go. It's knowing when to pause and when to keep going. The Lord has given us such a gift through prayer, and we don't want to miss it just because we are busy.

We will never be able to discern what everyone in our family needs. But God holds the keys to every heart. Through prayer you can ask Him to unlock the hearts of the ones you love.

 ## DROP-A-PIN VERSE

Call to me and I will answer you and tell you great and unsearchable things you do not know. Jeremiah 33:3

DIRECTION QUESTION

Where do you see God's glory in your family?

_____

_____

_____

PRAYER PROMPT

Ask the Lord for what His vision is for your family. Ask Him to give you eyes to see it in yourself and in those you love ... then watch for His movement.

_____

_____

_____

My children used to get concerned when they saw tears in my eyes. Once as we were preparing for the first day of school Benjamin saw my eyes glistening and said, "Mom, it makes me sad when you are sad; please don't cry."

It felt like the right time to explain something that has brought me great comfort as a mother. I let him know that many times, tears come from hearts that are breaking, but there are also times when tears come from hearts that are overflowing. Sometimes my tears are prayers my mouth can't speak. At that moment, my tears weren't from sadness; they were thanking the Lord for the gift of another wonderful summer together.

It is right and good that
our overflowing hearts are often
matched with overflowing eyes.

"So, son, each time you see a tear fall, you need to know this is my way of thanking the Lord. This tear says, 'Thank you for my son.' While this one says, 'I could not be prouder that he is mine.' Another one is saying, 'If we both live to be 200, I will never have enough time with him.' Don't let my tears make you sad, watch them fall and know I am so thankful to be your mom."

I know that my tears speak to the Lord in a way that my mouth cannot. Just as our God hears our voices, he also sees our tears. He knows why they fall, and he receives each one as a prayer from the deepest places of our heart. Some tears cry out for His help and intervention, while others offer a sincere form of praise

Tears are often a quiet way of praising God for this life He has so richly given. They are a mixture of joy and the sweetest of heartaches. These children are only in our homes for a season. It is right and good that our overflowing hearts are often matched with overflowing eyes.

YOU-ARE-HERE QUESTION

When was the last time your heart overflowed through your eyes?

_____

_____

_____

There are many ways to pray and bring your heart before the Lord. I used to get frustrated with my tears until I took Psalm 56:8 to heart: "You have collected all my tears in your bottle. You have recorded each one in your book" (NLT)

Knowing that the Lord keeps a record of each tear enabled me to embrace my tears as a heartfelt prayer for my children. Now, I offer my tears to the Lord. Being a mother has changed my prayer life. My children have brought Tony and me so much joy. But there has also been a lot of heartache.

Discipling children who think and love like Jesus is an admirable goal. Occasionally, there are points where you see glimpses of that goal being achieved. There will be moments you are proud of, moments you feel good about putting on social media, moments that make you feel like you are winning at this parenting gig. I love those moments, but it is helpful to remember there are also moments that feel like the pains of labor. There is no epidural for the exhaustion, ache, or uncertainty. Labor hurts.

In those times, recognize that you have a Helper unlike any other. He promises joy from mourning, beauty from ashes, strength from weakness, and so much more. Only God can assure that nothing is wasted.

Jesus doesn't just hear your prayers; He takes them and delivers them to your Heavenly Father. I believe Jesus is the One collecting our tears. He stays by your side, offering you what you need, even as He goes to the aid of your child. Your inability to see what is happening in the spiritual realm doesn't hinder God's ability to work in it.

Your heart may ask, "Are we making progress?"

Jesus answers, "Yes!" The pains of labor are moving you toward Jesus being formed in you and in your child.

Take heart! Your Deliverer is your child's as well. He is with you. He is with them. Fix your eyes on the goal.

Joy is coming.

 ## DROP-A-PIN VERSE

My dear children, I feel as if I am in labor pains for you again, and they will continue until Christ is formed in you.

Galatians 4:19 ESV

DIRECTION QUESTION

Where do you see yourself in labor for Christ to be formed in you? In your children?

_____

_____

_____

PRAYER PROMPT

Ask the Lord to continue to move you and your children closer to His heart. Ask that the character of Christ would continue to be formed in your family.

_____

_____

_____

Conclusion

*"I'm not saying that I have this all together, that I have
it made. But I am well on my way, reaching out
for Christ, who has so wondrously reached out for me.
Friends, don't get me wrong: By no means do I count myself
an expert in all of this, but I've got my eye on the goal,
where God is beckoning us onward—to Jesus.
I'm off and running, and I'm not turning back.
So let's keep focused on that goal, those of us
who want everything God has for us. If any of you have
something else in mind, something less than total commitment,
God will clear your blurred vision—you'll see it yet!
Now that we're on the right track, let's stay on it."*

Philippians 3:12-16 (MSG)

May the Lord continue to lead us as we navigate motherhood.

—Becky Brooks

ACKNOWLEDGMENTS

Many people helped me to make this book possible and I am forever grateful...

To Jamie Leat... The Lord gave you a vision for women, and you called the new class "Navigating Motherhood." As a result of the implementation of your vision thousands have come to know the Lord better in the midst of motherhood. Thank you for always believing in me.

To Anita Royse, Betty Martin, Jill Brazle, Beth Voss and Diane Wright ... Our original five mentoring moms. Because you five laid a strong foundation the work of the Lord has been able to grow. Thank you all for signing up and giving your hearts. So many mothers know Jesus better because they now know you.

To all the mentoring moms who have come after these five ... May God continue to bless you as you point others to him. What a gift it was to work alongside and be encouraged by you.

To Barbara Gradke ... Thank you for giving me the opportunity to teach and for gently pushing me to write. You reflect Jesus as you lead through service. May the Lord continue to grow your ministry. I will always be thankful for the years he gave us working side by side. You are close to my heart.

To Amanda Orr ... Without your weekly, "Do you have that lesson ready?" text, none of this would have happened. You stepped out in faith to teach and pushed me to write in the same way. I am forever thankful

To Suzanne Henley... You gave me a necklace that represented a mustard seed to remind me that you believed I would get this project accomplished. I have not taken it off. On days when I had to work hard to find words, that necklace was something I could touch and remember that faith, even when tiny, can do mighty things for the Lord.

To Liz Etheredge, Tina Clifton, Leah Kay Gabriel, Alexa Jaska, and Sarah Burk ... our 18 weeks together grew my faith and my heart for Jesus. I'm thankful to God that He brought us together and tangled our hearts. Thank you for every prayer. I treasure each of you.

To the Hills Church ... Thank you for the opportunity to teach and grow a program that revealed the Lord's heart to all of us. Thank you for blessing me at every turn. I saw and I see Jesus in your love. May the Lord continue to pour out His blessing on the body of Christ there.

To Megan Braswell, Cori Brown, Nathalie Hembree, June Paul, Staci Hutyra and Karissa Tolson ... Thank you for every encouraging text. The Holy Spirit in you always knew the exact moment I needed encouragement. Thank you for being faithful to give it.

To all my friends through the years, who have pressed and pushed in the gentlest of ways to make sure this project reached completion ... Thank you for encouraging, praying and saying "get to work" when I needed it most.

To Adrien Pekurney, Dereca Gist and Melissa McCasland ... Thank you for helping push me over the finish line in this project. I will forever be indebted. You went the extra mile, bringing meals, keeping my children, encouraging me until I said it was done. You believed in me when I was struggling. A friend who helps you start is great, but a friend who helps you finish is even better. I told each of you the burden I felt to write this book, and you helped me carry it until it was complete. Thank you for living out Galatians 6:2. The Lord is so good.

To Nika Maples … When the Lord put us together in 5th grade, He gave me such an incredible gift. Certainly I appreciated your friendship then, but now I realize the worth of the treasure. The Holy Spirit working through you and your gifts has shaped and molded this project into something that works. The Holy Spirit working through you and your gifts has shaped and molded me. Thank you for never giving up. Thank you for always coming when I call.

To my sister, Kelly Vaughn … You have been picking me up and putting me back on my feet since we were children. You are the one I call when I think perhaps I have said too much or too little. You are a wellspring of encouragement and a boost to my heart. I would have spent a lifetime looking for a friend like you, what a gift to be born your sister. You and Randy are a source of life and blessing to me.

To my brothers, Sam and Andy Jeffrey … My life has always felt more secure because you two are in it. Thanks for being friends I can count on and for marrying two of the best people I know. Emille and Jessica have brought a depth to our family that we were missing. Laughing with all of you is at the top of my list of favorite things.

To Mom and Dad … Thanks for listening to every lesson, for praying for me, and for challenging me in the Lord. Thank you for parenting us in a way that not only pointed to Jesus but also caused us to know Him as a friend. You showed us service and ministry was not an occupation but a way of life. Your children arise and call you blessed.

To Payton, Benjamin, Eden, and Shelby ... I'll never stop thanking the Lord for giving me a front row seat to your lives. Watching you grow and change and become who God created you to be is the joy of your dad's and my life together. The Lord writes the best stories and yours are my favorites.

To Tony ... Living and laughing with you is my heart's joy. Thanks for letting me share our life with others. Thanks for believing in me. I feel the Lord's smile when I see yours. A lifetime won't be long enough to love you.

Then to Jesus ... Thank You for giving me the words and the opportunity to speak them. Thank You for leading me through life and motherhood. I will spend the rest of my days serving You.

My heart is Yours.

Group Study

This book was written for individuals or groups. So much can be gained when mothers gather together with the sole purpose of encouraging each other.

We had great success with small groups being led by an older, more experienced mother. We called these our "mentoring moms." These women were vital in adding depth to this study and giving encouragement to every mom. What a gift for a mentor to remind a young mom, "God created you for this and you can do it."

If possible, please consider asking someone to serve as a mentoring mom to your group. The incredible blessing of being led and encouraged by someone a little further down the road of motherhood is life changing.

If you are able to gather a group. Consider these questions each week when you meet:

1. What stood out to you this week?
2. What are you doing differently in motherhood as a result of your study?
3. What *Drop-a-Pin* scripture are you letting anchor your heart?
4. How can this group hold you accountable to the change you are wanting to make?

To order *Navigating Motherhood* and other encouraging resources, please visit:

www.TheKeepGoingShop.com

COURAGE ALONG THE WAY

KEEP
GOING

365 DEVOTIONS

NIKA MAPLES

NOTES